The Broadview

POCKET GUIDE TO

Citation and Documentation

Third Edition

The Broadview
POCKET GUIDE TO
Citation and Documentation

Third Edition

Maureen Okun and Nora Ruddock

broadview press

BROADVIEW PRESS – www.broadviewpress.com
Peterborough, Ontario, Canada

Founded in 1985, Broadview Press remains a wholly independent publishing house. Broadview's focus is on academic publishing; our titles are accessible to university and college students as well as scholars and general readers. With over 800 titles in print, Broadview has become a leading international publisher in the humanities, with world-wide distribution. Broadview is committed to environmentally responsible publishing and fair business practices.

Library and Archives Canada Cataloguing in Publication
Title: The Broadview pocket guide to citation and documentation / Maureen Okun and Nora Ruddock.
Other titles: Pocket guide to citation and documentation
Names: Okun, Maureen, 1961- author. | Ruddock, Nora, 1978- author.
Description: Third edition. | Includes bibliographical references.
Identifiers: Canadiana (print) 20220211779 | Canadiana (ebook) 20220211809 |
    ISBN 9781554815227 (softcover) | ISBN 9781770488137 (PDF) |
    ISBN 9781460407622 (EPUB)
Subjects: LCSH: Bibliographical citations—Handbooks, manuals, etc. | LCSH: Academic
    writing—Handbooks, manuals, etc. | LCSH: Report writing—Handbooks, manuals, etc. |
    LCSH: Authorship—Style manuals. | LCSH: Authorship—Handbooks, manuals, etc. |
    LCGFT: Handbooks and manuals.
Classification: LCC PN171.F56 O48 2022 | DDC 808.02/7—dc23

Broadview Press handles its own distribution in North America
PO Box 1243, Peterborough, Ontario K9J 7H5, Canada
555 Riverwalk Parkway, Tonawanda, NY 14150, USA
Tel: (705) 743-8990; Fax: (705) 743-8353
email: customerservice@broadviewpress.com

For all territories outside of North America, distribution is handled by Eurospan Group.

Broadview Press acknowledges the financial support
of the Government of Canada
for our publishing activities.

Design and typeset by Eileen Eckert
Cover design by Lisa Brawn

PRINTED IN CANADA

CONTENTS

Documentation and Research 11

Avoiding Plagiarism—and Choosing When and What to Quote 12
Citation and Documentation 15
Incorporating Sources 16
  Summarizing 17
  Paraphrasing 18
  Quoting Directly 20
    Formatting Quotations 21
      Short Prose Quotations 21
      Long Prose Quotations 22
      Verse Quotations 23
      Quotations within Quotations 24
      Adding to or Deleting from a Quotation 25
        Using square brackets to add to a quotation 25
        Using an ellipsis to delete from a quotation 25
      Integrating Quotations 26
        Avoiding "dumped" quotations 27
  Signal Phrases 28

MLA Style 31

About In-Text Citations 33
  1. in-text citations 33
  2. no signal phrase 34
  3. placing of in-text citations 34
  4. in-text citation when text is in parentheses 35
  5. page number unavailable 35
  6. one page or less 36
  7. multiple authors 36
  8. corporate author 36
  9. more than one work by the same author cited 37
  10. multi-volume works 38
  11. two or more authors with the same last name 38
  12. indirect quotations 38
  13. short poems 39
  14. longer poems 39

Contents

15. novels or short stories 39
16. plays 40
17. works without page numbers............................. 41
18. sacred texts 41
19. works in an anthology or book of readings 42
20. tweets 42
About Works Cited 42
    MLA Core Elements 42
- Author.. 44
- Title of Source.. 48
- Title of Container 51
- Contributor... 56
- Version 57
- Number 58
- Publisher... 59
- Publication Date 60
- Location 63
    Supplemental Elements 65
- Date of Original Publication............................ 65
- City of Publication 65
- Books in a Series 66
- Unexpected Type of Work............................... 66
- Date of Access... 66
    Examples 67
21. single author 67
22. two authors... 67
23. three or more authors 67
24. corporate author 68
25. works with an anonymous author 68
26. two or more works by the same author 68
27. works under a pseudonym............................... 68
28. edited works 69
29. works in translation.................................... 69
30. selections from anthologies or collections of readings 69
31. cross-references for works from the same collection or anthology 70
32. multi-volume works 70
33. different editions...................................... 71
34. republished sources 71
35. reference work entries 72
36. works with a title in the title 72

37. material from prefaces, introductions, etc. 73
38. magazine articles 73
39. newspaper articles 74
40. journal articles. 75
41. book reviews 75
42. periodical publications in online databases .76
43. illustrated books 76
44. graphic narratives 76
45. films or television episodes 77
46. online videos. 77
47. radio broadcasts. 78
48. podcasts. 78
49. recorded music 78
50. live performances. 78
51. works of visual art 79
52. interviews 79
53. online projects. 80
54. e-books 80
55. information databases 81
56. entry in a wiki 81
57. blog post 81
58. e-mail message. 82
59. tweet 82
60. comment posted on a webpage 82
MLA Style Sample Essay. 84

APA Style 121

Incorporating Sources in APA Style. 123
    Summarizing. 124
    Paraphrasing 125
    Quoting Directly. 127
        Formatting Quotations 128
            Short Quotations 128
            Long Quotations. 129
            Quotations within Quotations 130
            Adding to or Deleting from a Quotation. 130
                Using square brackets to add to a quotation 131
                Using an ellipsis to delete from a quotation. 131
            Integrating Quotations 132

Contents

  Avoiding "dumped" quotations 132
 Signal Phrases 133
About In-Text Citations 135
 1. in-text citation 135
 2. no signal phrase (or author not named in signal phrase) 137
 3. titles of stand-alone works 137
 4. titles of articles and chapters of books 138
 5. placing of in-text citations 138
 6. citations when text is in parentheses 139
 7. electronic source—page number unavailable 139
 8. audiovisual works 140
 9. two or more dates for a work 140
 10. two authors 141
 11. three or more authors 141
 12. organization as author 142
 13. author not given 142
 14. date not given 142
 15. two or more works in the same citation 142
 16. two or more authors with the same last name 143
 17. works in a collection of readings or anthology 143
 18. indirect source 144
 19. personal communications 145
 20. Indigenous traditional knowledge and oral traditions 145
About References 146
 21. work with single author 148
 22. two authors 148
 23. three to twenty authors 148
 24. more than twenty authors 149
 25. works with an organization as author 149
 26. works with unknown author 149
 27. two or more works by the same author 150
 28. two or more works by the same author in the same year 150
 29. prefaces, introductions, forewords, afterwords 151
 30. edited works 151
 31. works with an author and a translator 151
 32. selections from edited books and collections of readings 151
 33. selections from multivolume works 152
 34. ebooks and audiobooks 152
 35. periodical articles (with and without DOIs) 152
 36. abstract of a periodical article 154

37. magazine articles 154
38. newspaper articles 154
39. reviews 155
40. reference work entries with an individual author 155
41. reference work entries with an organization as author 155
42. diagnostic manuals (DSM and ICD). 156
43. articles from databases. . . . . . .'. 156
44. dissertations from databases, published and unpublished. 157
45. data sets. 158
46. software and reference apps 158
47. films and video recordings. 158
48. episodes from television series 159
49. TED talks . . . . ; 159
50. YouTube and other streaming videos 159
51. podcasts. 160
52. music recordings 160
53. recorded webinars 161
54. interviews 161
55. blog posts 161
56. Wikipedia article. 162
57. social media. 162
58. Facebook posts 163
59. Instagram photos or videos 163
60. tweets 163
61. other webpages and websites 164
62. visual works. 164
63. work of art in a gallery or gallery website. 164
64. stock images or clip art 165
65. infographics. 165
66. maps 165
67. photographs 165
68. PowerPoint slides, lecture notes, recorded Zoom lectures. 166
69. conference presentations 166
APA Style Sample Essay. 168

Chicago Style 185
About Chicago Style 187
1. notes 188
2. titles: italics/quotation marks. 189
3. multiple references to the same work. 190

4. page number or date unavailable..................................190
5. two or more dates for a work.................................192
6. two or three authors 193
7. four or more authors......................................193
8. organization as author/reference work/government document 193
9. works from a collection of readings or anthology................195
10. indirect source...196
11. two or more works by the same author 196
12. edited works 196
13. translated works 197
14. e-books 197
15. magazine articles.......................................198
16. newspaper articles......................................199
17. journal articles...199
18. films and video recordings.................................200
19. television broadcasts 201
20. sound recordings.......................................201
21. interviews and personal communications 202
22. book reviews 203
23. blog posts 203
24. websites...203
25. online videos...204
26. tweets 204
Chicago Style Sample 206

CSE Style 213

In-Text Citation 213
    citation-name format...................................213
    citation-sequence format................................214
    name-year format 214
List of References 214
    citation-name format...................................214
    citation-sequence format................................215
    name-year format 215
CSE Style Samples 217
    citation-name format...................................217
    citation-sequence format................................221
    name-year format 225

◉ DOCUMENTATION AND RESEARCH

Writers have a variety of reasons for including the results of research in their essays. Outside sources can help support or clarify authors' points, or can provide opposing arguments against which authors can make their own case. Sources are also useful in showing where a paper can be located in the wider conversation among writers engaged by the same subject. At the very least, including source material is one way writers can show that they are acquainted with the latest thinking on their topics.

Whatever the reasons for incorporating research into their essays, good writers are careful in how they do so, making sure to document their sources accurately and completely. This is, first of all, a service to readers who would like to embark on a fuller investigation into the topic of a paper by looking up its sources themselves; every academic citation system gives readers all the information they need to access original source material. But it is also critical that there be complete clarity about which parts of an essay are the author's and which parts come from elsewhere. To allow any blurriness on this question is to be dishonest, to engage in a kind of cheating, in fact—known as plagiarism.

Documentation
and Research

O *Avoiding Plagiarism—and Choosing When and What to Quote*

Most people understand that taking someone else's writing and passing it off as one's own is intellectual thievery. But it is important to be aware that you may commit plagiarism even if you do not use precisely the same words another person wrote in precisely the same order. For instance, here is an actual example of plagiarism. *Globe and Mail* newspaper columnist Margaret Wente borrowed material for one of her columns from a number of works, including an article by Dan Gardner that had appeared the previous year in another newspaper (the *Ottawa Citizen*) and a book by Robert Paarlberg called *Starved for Science* (which was the subject of Gardner's article). The similarities were brought to light by media commentator Carol Wainio, who presented a series of parallel passages, including the following, on her blog *Media Culpa* (the fonts are Wainio's—simple bold is for direct copying; the bold + italics is for "near copying"):

> Gardner: ***Many NGOs working in Africa in the area of development and the environment have been advocating against the modernization of traditional farming practices***, Paarlberg says. "**They believe that traditional farming in Africa incorporates indigenous knowledge that shouldn't be replaced by science-based knowledge introduced from the outside.** They encourage Africa to stay away from fertilizers, and be certified as organic instead. And in the case of genetic engineering, they warn African governments against making these technologies available to farmers."

Wente: ***Yet, many NGOs working in Africa have tenaciously fought the modernization of traditional farming practices. They believe traditional farming in Africa incorporates indigenous knowledge that shouldn't be replaced by science-based knowledge introduced from the outside.*** As Prof. Paarlberg writes, "They encourage African farmers to stay away from fertilizers and be certified organic instead. And they warn African governments to stay away from genetic engineering."

Wente does not always use exactly the same words as her sources, but no one reading the passages can doubt that one writer is appropriating the phrasings of the others. Additionally, where Wente *does* quote Paarlberg directly, the quotation is lifted from Gardner's article and should be identified as such.

The penalties for such practices are not trivial; Wente was publicly reprimanded by her employer, and the CBC radio program *Q* removed her from its media panel. Other reporters have been, justifiably, fired under similar circumstances. At most colleges and universities, students are likely to receive a zero if they are caught plagiarizing—and they may be expelled from the institution. It's important to be aware, too, that penalties for plagiarism make no allowance for intent; it is no defense that a writer took someone else's words "by mistake" rather than intentionally.

How, then, can you be sure to avoid plagiarism? First of all, be extremely careful in your note-taking, so as to make it impossible to imagine, a few days later, that words you have jotted down from somewhere else are your own. This is why notes need to be in a separate file or book from your own ideas. (In her *Globe and Mail* column responding to the plagiarism charges, Wente, in fact, claimed that she had accidentally mixed a quotation into her own ideas.) If your note-taking is reliable, then you will know which words need to be credited. One way to rewrite the passage above would simply be to remove the material taken from Gardner and to credit Paarlberg by quoting him directly, if you were able to access his book and could do so: "As Robert Paarlberg has argued in his book *Starved for Science*, many NGOs 'believe that traditional farming in Africa incorporates indigenous knowledge that shouldn't be replaced by science-based knowledge introduced from the outside.'" You would, of course, find and provide the page number as well.

You may notice that the quoted material is a statement of opinion rather than fact—controversial views are being given, but without any evidence provided to back them up—so a careful reader would wonder whether NGOs are really as anti-science as the quotation suggests, or whether the writer hasn't done enough research on the debate. If you were to make an assertion like this in a paper of your own it would not be enough just to quote Paarlberg; you would need to do much more research and find information to support or deny your claim. If you are including quotations in an essay, the best sources to quote are not necessarily those which express opinions that mirror the ones you are putting forward. In a case such as this, for example, the argument would have been much more persuasive if Wente had quoted an official statement from one of the NGOs she was attacking. If her article had quoted a source making this specific case against "science-based knowledge" and then argued directly against that source's argument, Wente's own position would have been strengthened. Quoting many such sources would provide proof that the article's characterization of the position of NGOs was factually accurate.

Whenever you do quote someone else, it's important to cite the source. But do you need a citation for everything that did not come from your own knowledge? Not necessarily. Citations are usually unnecessary when you are touching on common knowledge (provided it is, in fact, common knowledge, and provided your instructor has not asked you to do otherwise). If you refer to the chemical composition of water, or the date when penicillin was discovered, you are unlikely to need to provide any citation, even if you used a source to find the information, since such facts are generally available and uncontroversial. (Make sure, however, to check any "common knowledge" with several reputable sources; if your information is incorrect, it reflects poorly on you, especially if you have not cited your source.) If you have any doubts about whether something is common knowledge or not, cite it; over-cautiousness is not a serious problem, but plagiarism always is.

O *Citation and Documentation*

Citing sources is fundamental to writing a good research paper, but no matter how diligent you are in making your acknowledgments, your paper will not be taken seriously unless its documentation is formatted according to an appropriate and accepted referencing style. For the sake of consistency, each academic discipline has adopted a particular system of referencing as its standard, which those writing in that discipline are expected to follow. *The Broad-*

view Pocket Guide to Citation and Documentation outlines the four most common of these systems. Almost all of the humanities use the documentation guidelines developed by the Modern Language Association (MLA), a notable exception being history, which tends to prefer those of the *Chicago Manual of Style* (Chicago Style). The social and some health sciences typically follow the style rules of the American Psychological Association (APA), while the basic sciences most commonly use the referencing systems of the Council of Science Editors (CSE). Each of these styles is exacting and comprehensive in its formatting rules; following with precision the one recommended for a given paper's discipline is one of a responsible research writer's duties. Details of these systems are in the pages that follow.

As important as documentation is to a well-written paper, by itself it is not always enough. Writers must also be attentive to the ways in which they integrate borrowed material into their essays.

O *Incorporating Sources*

There are three main ways of working source material into a paper: summarizing, paraphrasing, and quoting directly. In order to avoid plagiarism, care must be taken with all three kinds of borrowing, both in the way they are handled and in their referencing. In what follows, a passage from page 102 of a book by Terrence W. Deacon (*The Symbolic Species: The Co-Evolution of Language and the Brain*) serves as the source for a sample summary, paraphrase, and quotation. The examples feature the MLA style of in-text parenthetical citations, but the requirements for presenting the source material are the same for all academic referencing systems. For a similar discussion with a focus on APA style, see Incorporating Sources in APA Style (starting on page 123).

original source   Over the last few decades language researchers seem to have reached a consensus that language is an innate ability, and that only a significant contribution from innate knowledge can explain our ability to learn such a complex communication system. Without question, children enter the world predisposed to learn human languages. All normal children, raised in normal social environments, inevitably learn their local language, whereas other species, even when raised and taught in this same environment, do not. This demonstrates that human brains come into the world specially equipped for this function.

O *Summarizing*

An honest and competent summary, whether of a passage or an entire book, must not only represent the source accurately but also use original wording and include a citation. It is a common misconception that only quotations need to be acknowledged as borrowings in the body of an essay. In fact, without a citation, even a fairly worded summary or paraphrase is an act of plagiarism. The first example below is faulty on two counts: it borrows wording (underlined) from the source, and it has no parenthetical reference.

needs checking   <u>Researchers</u> agree that language learning is <u>innate, and that only innate knowledge can explain</u> how we are able <u>to learn</u> a <u>system</u> of <u>communication</u> that is so <u>complex</u>. <u>Normal children raised in normal</u> ways will always <u>learn their local language, whereas other species do not, even when taught</u> human language and exposed to the <u>same environment</u>.

The next example correctly avoids the wording of the source passage, and a signal phrase and parenthetical citation note the author and page number.

revised   As Terrence W. Deacon notes, there is now wide agreement among linguists that the ease with which human children acquire their native tongues, under the conditions of a normal childhood, demonstrates an inborn capacity for language that is not shared by any other animals, not even those who are reared in comparable ways and given human language training (102).

O *Paraphrasing*

Whereas a summary is a shorter version of its original, a paraphrase tends to be about the same length. However, paraphrases, just like summaries, must reflect their sources accurately, must use original wording, and must include a citation. Even though it is properly cited, the paraphrase of the first sentence of the Deacon passage, below, falls short by being too close to the wording of the original (underlined).

needs checking <u>Researchers</u> in <u>language</u> have come to <u>a consen-</u>
<u>sus</u> in the past <u>few decades</u> that the acquisition
of language is <u>innate</u>; such <u>contributions</u> <u>from</u>
<u>knowledge</u> <u>contribute significantly</u> to <u>our abil-</u>
<u>ity</u> to master <u>such a complex system</u> of <u>com-</u>
<u>munication</u> (Deacon 102).

Simply substituting synonyms for the words and phrases
of the source, however, is not enough to avoid plagiarism.
Despite its original wording, the next example also fails but
for a very different reason: it follows the original's sentence
structure too closely, as illustrated in the interpolated copy
below it.

needs checking Recently, linguists appear to have come to an
agreement that speaking is an inborn skill,
and that nothing but a substantial input from
inborn cognition can account for the human
capacity to acquire such a complicated means
of expression (Deacon 102).

Recently (*over the last few decades*), linguists
(*language researchers*) appear to have come to
an agreement (*seem to have reached a consensus*)
that speaking is an inborn skill (*that language is
an innate ability*), and that nothing but a substantial input (*and that only a significant contribution*) from inborn cognition (*from innate
knowledge*) can account for the human capacity
(*can explain our ability*) to acquire such a complicated means of expression (*to learn such a
complex communication system*) (Deacon 102).

What follows is a good paraphrase of the passage's opening sentence; this paraphrase captures the sense of the original without echoing the details and shape of its language.

> *revised*   Linguists now broadly agree that children are born with the ability to learn language; in fact, the human capacity to acquire such a difficult skill cannot easily be accounted for in any other way (Deacon 102).

O *Quoting Directly*

Unlike paraphrases and summaries, direct quotations must use the exact wording of the original. Because they involve importing outside words, quotations pose unique challenges. Quote too frequently, and you risk making your readers wonder why they are not reading your sources instead of your paper. Your essay should present something you want to say—informed and supported by properly documented sources, but forming a contribution that is yours alone. To that end, use secondary material to help you build a strong framework for your work, not to replace it. Quote sparingly, therefore; use your sources' exact wording only when it is important or particularly memorable.

To avoid misrepresenting your sources, be sure to quote accurately, and to avoid plagiarism, take care to indicate quotations as quotations, and cite them properly. Below are two problematic quotations. The first does not show which words come directly from the source.

needs checking   Terrence W. Deacon maintains that children enter the world predisposed to learn human languages (102).

The second quotation fails to identify the source at all.

needs checking   Linguists believe that "children enter the world predisposed to learn human languages."

The next example corrects both problems by naming the source and indicating clearly which words come directly from it.

revised   Terrence W. Deacon maintains that "children enter the world predisposed to learn human languages" (102).

◎ Formatting Quotations

There are two ways to signal an exact borrowing: by enclosing it in double quotation marks and by indenting it as a block of text. Which you should choose depends on the length and genre of the quotation and the style guide you are following.

⊙ Short Prose Quotations

What counts as a short prose quotation differs among the various reference guides. In MLA style, "short" means up to four lines; in APA, up to forty words; and in Chicago Style, up to one hundred words. All the guides agree, however, that short quotations must be enclosed in double quotation marks, as in the examples below.

Short quotation, full sentence:
According to Terrence W. Deacon, linguists agree that a human child's capacity to acquire language is inborn: "Without question, children enter the world predisposed to learn human languages" (102).

Short quotation, partial sentence:
According to Terrence W. Deacon, linguists agree that human "children enter the world predisposed to learn human languages" (102).

Documentation and Research

⊙ Long Prose Quotations

Longer prose quotations should be double-spaced and indented, as a block, one tab space from the left margin. Do not include quotation marks; the indentation indicates that the words come exactly from the source. Note that indented quotations are often introduced with a full sentence followed by a colon.

> Terrence W. Deacon, like most other linguists, believes that human beings are born with a unique cognitive capacity:
>
> > Without question, children enter the world predisposed to learn human languages. All normal children, raised in normal social environments, inevitably learn their local language, whereas other species, even when raised and taught in this same environment, do not. This demonstrates that human brains come into the world specially equipped for this function. (102)

⊙ Verse Quotations

Quoting from verse is a special case. Poetry quotations of three or fewer lines (MLA) may be integrated into your paragraph and enclosed in double quotation marks, with lines separated by a forward slash with a space on either side of it, as in the example below.

> Pope's "Epistle II. To a Lady," in its vivid portrayal of wasted lives, sharply criticizes the social values that render older women superfluous objects of contempt: "Still round and round the Ghosts of Beauty glide, / And haunt the places where their Honor dy'd" (lines 241–42).

If your quotation of three or fewer lines includes a stanza break, MLA style requires you to mark the break by inserting two forward slashes (//), with spaces on either side of them.

> The speaker in "Ode to a Nightingale" seeks, in various ways, to free himself from human consciousness, leaving suffering behind. Keats uses alliteration and repetition to mimic the gradual dissolution of self, the process of intoxication or death: "That I might drink, and leave the world unseen, / And with thee fade away into the forest dim: // Fade far away, dissolve, and quite forget" (lines 19–21).

Poetry quotations of more than three lines in MLA, or two or more lines in Chicago Style, should be indented and set off in a block from your main text. Arrange the lines just as they appear in the original.

The ending of Margaret Avison's "September Street" moves from the decaying, discordant city toward a glimpse of an outer/inner infinitude:

> On the yellow porch
> one sits, not reading headlines; the old eyes
>   read far out into the mild
>   air, runes.
> See. There: a stray sea-gull. (lines 20–24)

⊙ Quotations within Quotations

You may sometimes find, within the original passage you wish to quote, words already enclosed in double quotation marks. If your quotation is short, enclose it all in double quotation marks, and use single quotation marks for the embedded quotation.

> Terrence W. Deacon is firm in maintaining that human language differs from other communication systems in kind rather than degree: "Of no other natural form of communication is it legitimate to say that 'language is a more complicated version of that'" (44).

If your quotation is long, keep the double quotation marks of the original.

> Terrence W. Deacon is firm in maintaining that human language differs from other communication systems in kind rather than degree:
>
> > Of no other natural form of communication is it legitimate to say that "language is a more compli-cated version of that." It is just as misleading to

call other species' communication systems *simple* languages as it is to call them languages. In addition to asserting that a Procrustean mapping of one to the other is possible, the analogy ignores the sophistication and power of animals' non-linguistic communication, whose capabilities may also be without language parallels. (44)

⊙ Adding to or Deleting from a Quotation

While it is important to use the original's exact wording in a quotation, it is allowable to modify a quotation somewhat, as long as the changes are clearly indicated and do not distort the meaning of the original.

● *Using square brackets to add to a quotation*

You may want to add to a quotation in order to clarify what would otherwise be puzzling or ambiguous to someone who does not know its context; in that case, put whatever you add in square brackets.

Terrence W. Deacon writes that children are born "specially equipped for this [language] function" (102).

● *Using an ellipsis to delete from a quotation*

If you would like to streamline a quotation by omitting anything unnecessary to your point, insert an ellipsis (three spaced dots) to show that you've left material out.

When the quotation looks like a complete sentence but is actually part of a longer sentence, you should provide an ellipsis to show that there is more to the original than you are using.

> Terrence W. Deacon says that ". . . children enter the world predisposed to learn human languages" (102).

Note that if the quotation is clearly a partial sentence, ellipses aren't necessary.

> Terrence W. Deacon writes that children are born "specially equipped" to learn human language (102).

When the omitted material runs over a sentence boundary or constitutes a whole sentence or more, insert a period plus an ellipsis.

> Terrence W. Deacon, like most other linguists, believes that human children are born with a unique ability to acquire their native language: "Without question, children enter the world predisposed to learn human languages. . . . [H]uman brains come into the world specially equipped for this function" (102).

Be sparing in modifying quotations; it is all right to have one or two altered quotations in a paper, but if you find yourself changing quotations often, or adding to and omitting from one quotation more than once, reconsider quoting at all. A paraphrase or summary is very often a more effective choice.

⊙ Integrating Quotations

Quotations must be worked smoothly and grammatically into your sentences and paragraphs. Always, of course, mark quotations as such, but for the purpose of integrating them into your writing, treat them as if they were your own words. The boundary between what you say and what your source says should be grammatically seamless.

needs checking Terrence W. Deacon points out, "whereas other species, even when raised and taught in this same environment, do not" (102).

revised According to Terrence W. Deacon, while human children brought up under normal conditions acquire the language they are exposed to, "other species, even when raised and taught in this same environment, do not" (102).

⊙ *Avoiding "dumped" quotations*

Integrating quotations well also means providing a context for them. Don't merely drop them into your paper or string them together like beads on a necklace; make sure to introduce them by noting where the material comes from and how it connects to whatever point you are making.

needs checking For many years, linguists have studied how human children acquire language. "Without question, children enter the world predisposed to learn human language" (Deacon 102).

revised Most linguists studying how human children acquire language have come to share the conclusion articulated here by Terrence W. Deacon: "Without question, children enter the world predisposed to learn human language" (102).

Documentation and Research

needs checking   "Without question, children enter the world predisposed to learn human language" (Deacon 102). "There is . . . something special about human brains that enables us to do with ease what no other species can do even minimally without intense effort and remarkably insightful training" (Deacon 103).

revised   Terrence W. Deacon bases his claim that we "enter the world predisposed to learn human language" on the fact that very young humans can "do with ease what no other species can do even minimally without intense effort and remarkably insightful training" (102–03).

○ Signal Phrases

To leave no doubt in your readers' minds about which parts of your essay are yours and which come from elsewhere, identify the sources of your summaries, paraphrases, and quotations with signal phrases, as in the following examples.

- As Carter and Rosenthal have demonstrated, . . .
- In the words of one researcher, . . .
- In his most recent book McGann advances the view that, as he puts it, . . .
- As Nussbaum observes, . . .
- Kendal suggests that . . .
- Freschi and other scholars have rejected these claims, arguing that . . .
- Morgan has emphasized this point in her recent research: . . .
- As Sacks puts it, . . .

- To be sure, Mtele allows that . . .
- In his later novels Hardy takes a bleaker view, frequently suggesting that . . .

In order to help establish your paper's credibility, you may also find it useful at times to include in a signal phrase information that shows why readers should take the source seriously, as in the following example:

> In her landmark work, biologist and conservationist Rachel Carson warns that . . .

Here, the signal phrase mentions the author's professional credentials; it also points out the importance of her book, which is appropriate to do in the case of a work as famous as Carson's *Silent Spring*.

Below is a fuller list of words and expressions that may be useful in the crafting of signal phrases:

according to _____,	endorses
acknowledges	finds
adds	grants
admits	illustrates
advances	implies
agrees	in the view of _____,
allows	in the words of _____,
argues	insists
asserts	intimates
attests	notes
believes	observes
claims	points out
comments	puts it
compares	reasons
concludes	refutes
confirms	rejects
contends	reports
declares	responds
demonstrates	suggests
denies	takes issue with
disputes	thinks
emphasizes	writes

MLA Style

About In-Text Citations   33

   1.   in-text citations   33
   2.   no signal phrase   34
   3.   placing of in-text citations   34
   4.   in-text citation when text is in parentheses   35
   5.   page number unavailable   35
   6.   one page or less   36
   7.   multiple authors   36
   8.   corporate author   36
   9.   more than one work by the same author cited   37
 10.   multi-volume works   38
 11.   two or more authors with the same last name   38
 12.   indirect quotations   38
 13.   short poems   39
 14.   longer poems   39
 15.   novels or short stories   39
 16.   plays   40
 17.   works without page numbers   41
 18.   sacred texts   41
 19.   works in an anthology or book of readings   42
 20.   tweets   42

About Works Cited   42

MLA Core Elements   42

  • Author   44
  • Title of Source   48
  • Title of Container   51
  • Contributor   56
  • Version   57
  • Number   58
  • Publisher   59
  • Publication Date   60
  • Location   63

Supplemental Elements   65

  • Date of Original Publication   65
  • City of Publication   65
  • Books in a Series   66
  • Unexpected Type of Work   66
  • Date of Access   66

MLA Style

Examples 67
21. single author 67
22. two authors 67
23. three or more authors 67
24. corporate author 68
25. works with an anonymous author 68
26. two or more works by the same author 68
27. works under a pseudonym 68
28. edited works 69
29. works in translation 69
30. selections from anthologies or collections of readings 69
31. cross-references for works from the same collection or anthology 70
32. multi-volume works 70
33. different editions 71
34. republished sources 71
35. reference work entries 72
36. works with a title in the title 72
37. material from prefaces, introductions, etc. 73
38. magazine articles 73
39. newspaper articles 74
40. journal articles 75
41. book reviews 75
42. periodical publications in online databases 76
43. illustrated books 76
44. graphic narratives 76
45. films or television episodes 77
46. online videos 77
47. radio broadcasts 78
48. podcasts 78
49. recorded music 78
50. live performances 78
51. works of visual art 79
52. interviews 79
53. online projects 80
54. e-books 80
55. information databases 81
56. entry in a wiki 81
57. blog post 81
58. e-mail message 82
59. tweet 82
60. comment posted on a webpage 82

MLA Style Sample Essay 85

◎ MLA Style

"MLA style" refers to the referencing guidelines of the Modern Language Association, which are favored by many disciplines in the humanities. The main components of the MLA system are in-text author-page number citations for the body of an essay, and a bibliography giving publication details—the list of "Works Cited"—at the end of it.

This section outlines the key points of MLA style. A full-length sample essay appears at the end of this section, and additional sample essays can be found on the Broadview writing website; go to sites.broadviewpress.com/writing. Consult the *MLA Handbook* (9th edition, 2021) if you have questions not answered here; you may also find answers at the website of the MLA, www.mla.org, where updates and answers to frequently asked questions are posted.

O *About In-Text Citations*

1. in-text citations: Under the MLA system a quotation or specific reference to another work is followed by a parenthetical page reference:

- Bonnycastle refers to "the true and lively spirit of opposition" with which Marxist literary criticism invigorates the discipline (204).

The work is then listed under "Works Cited" at the end of the essay:

- Bonnycastle, Stephen. *In Search of Authority: An Introductory Guide to Literary Theory*. 3rd ed., Broadview Press, 2007.

(See below for information about the "Works Cited" list.)

2. no signal phrase (or author not named in signal phrase): If the context does not make clear who the author is, that information must be added to the in-text citation. Note that no comma separates the name of the author from the page number.

- Even in recent years some have continued to believe that Marxist literary criticism invigorates the discipline with a "true and lively spirit of opposition" (Bonnycastle 204).

3. placing of in-text citations: Place in-text citations at the ends of clauses or sentences in order to keep disruption of your writing to a minimum. The citation comes before the period or comma in the surrounding sentence. (If the quotation ends with punctuation other than a period or comma, include it in the quotation, and place a period or comma after the in-text citation.)

- Ricks refuted this point early on (16), but the claim has continued to be made in recent years.
- In "The Windhover," on the other hand, Hopkins bubbles over; "the mastery of the thing!" (8), he enthuses when he thinks of a bird, exclaiming shortly thereafter, "O my chevalier!" (10).

When a cited quotation is set off from the text, however, the in-text citation should be placed after the concluding punctuation.

- Muriel Jaeger draws on the following anecdote in discussing the resistance of many wealthy Victorians to the idea of widespread education for the poor:

> In a mischievous mood, Henry Brougham once told [some well-off acquaintances who were] showing perturbation about the likely results of educating the "lower orders" that they could maintain their superiority by working harder themselves. (105)

4. in-text citation when text is in parentheses: If an in-text citation occurs within text in parentheses, square brackets are used for the reference.

- The development of a mass literary culture (or a "print culture," to use Williams's expression [88]) took several hundred years in Britain.

5. page number unavailable: Many web sources lack page numbers. If your source has no page or section numbers, no number should be given in your citation. Do not count paragraphs yourself, as the version you are using may differ from others.

- In a recent web posting a leading critic has clearly implied that he finds such an approach objectionable (Bhabha).

If the source gives explicit paragraph or section numbers, as many websites do, cite the appropriate abbreviation, followed by the number.

- Early in the novel, Austen makes it clear that the "business" of Mrs. Bennet's life is "to get her daughters married" (ch. 1).

- In "The American Scholar" Emerson asserts that America's "long apprenticeship to the learning of other lands" is drawing to a close (par. 7).

MLA Style

Note that (as is not the case with page numbers) MLA style requires a comma between author and paragraph or section numbers in a citation.

- Early in the novel, Mrs. Bennet makes it clear that her sole business in life is "to get her daughters married" (Austen, ch. 1).

6. one page or less: If a source is one page long or less, it is advisable to still provide the page number (though MLA does not require this).

- In his *Chicago Tribune* review, Bosley calls the novel's prose "excruciating" (1).

7. multiple authors: If there are two authors, both authors should be named either in the signal phrase or in the in-text citation, connected by *and*.

- Chambliss and Best argue that the importance of this novel is primarily historical (233).

- Two distinguished scholars have recently argued that the importance of this novel is primarily historical (Chambliss and Best 233).

If there are three or more authors, include only the first author's name in the in-text citation, followed by *et al.*, short for the Latin *et alia*, meaning *and others*.

- Meaning is not simply there in the text, but in the complex relationships between the text, the reader, and the Medieval world (Black et al. xxxvi).

8. corporate author: The relevant organization or the title of the piece should be included in the in-text citation if neither is included in the body of your text; make sure enough information is provided for readers to find the correct entry in your Works Cited list. Shorten a long title to avoid awkwardness, but take care that the shortened version begins with the same word as the corresponding entry in the "Works Cited" list, so that readers can move easily from the citation to the bibliographic information. For example, *Comparative Indo-European Linguistics: An Introduction* should be shortened to *Comparative Indo-European* rather than *Indo-European Linguistics*. The first two examples below cite unsigned newspaper and encyclopedia articles; the last is a corporate author in-text citation.

- As *The New York Times* reported in May 2021, many of the new voting laws being enacted were driven by disinformation about election integrity ("Perpetual Motion Machine").

- In the 1990s Sao Paulo began to rapidly overtake Mexico City as the world's most polluted city ("Air Pollution" 21).

- There are a number of organizations mandated "to foster the production and enjoyment of the arts in Canada" (Canada Council for the Arts 2).

9. more than one work by the same author cited: If you include more than one work by the same author in your list of Works Cited, you must make clear which work is being cited each time. This may be done either by mentioning the work in a signal phrase or by including in the citation a short version of the title.

- In *The House of Mirth*, for example, Wharton writes of love as keeping Lily and Selden "from atrophy and extinction" (282).

- Wharton sees love as possessing the power to keep humans "from atrophy and extinction" (*House of Mirth* 282).

- Love, as we learn from the experience of Lily and Selden, possesses the power to keep humans "from atrophy and extinction" (Wharton, *House of Mirth* 282).

10. multi-volume works: Note, by number, the volume you are referring to, followed by a colon and a space, before noting the page number. Use the abbreviation "vol." when citing an entire volume.

- Towards the end of *In Darkest Africa* Stanley refers to the Victoria Falls (2: 387).

- In contrast with those of the medieval period, Renaissance artworks show an increasing concern with depicting the material world and less and less of an interest in metaphysical symbolism (Hauser, vol. 2).

11. two or more authors with the same last name: If the Works Cited list includes two or more authors with the same last name, the in-text citation should supply both first initials and last names, or, if the first initials are also the same, the full first and last names:

- One of the leading economists of the time advocated wage and price controls (Harry Johnston 197).

- One of the leading economists of the time advocated wage and price controls (H. Johnston 197).

12. indirect quotations: When an original source is not available but is referred to by another source, the in-text citation includes *qtd. in* (an abbreviation of *quoted in*) and a reference to the second source. In the example below, Casewell is quoted by Bouvier; the in-text citation directs readers to an entry in the Works Cited list for the Bouvier work.

- Casewell considers Lambert's position to be "outrageously arrogant" (qtd. in Bouvier 59).

13. short poems: For short poems, cite line numbers rather than page numbers.

- In "won't you celebrate with me," Clifton describes a speaker who forges her identity "here on this bridge between / starshine and clay" (lines 8–9).

If you are citing the same poem repeatedly, use just the numbers for subsequent references.

- Clifton asks the reader to celebrate that "everyday / something has tried to kill me / and has failed" (12–14).

14. longer poems: For longer poems with parts, cite the part (or section, or "book") as well as the line (where available). Use Arabic numerals, and use a period for separation.

- In "Ode: Intimations of Immortality" Wordsworth calls human birth "but a sleep and a forgetting" (5.1).

15. novels or short stories: When a work of prose fiction has chapters or numbered divisions the citation should include first the page number, and then book, chapter, and section numbers as applicable. (These can be very useful in helping readers of a different edition to locate the passage you are citing.) Arabic numerals should be used. A semicolon should be used to separate the page number from the other information.

- When Joseph and Fanny are by themselves, they immediately express their affection for each other, or, as Fielding puts it, "solace themselves" with "amorous discourse" (151; ch. 26).

- In *Tender Is the Night* Dick's ambition does not quite crowd out the desire for love: "He wanted to be loved too, if he could fit it in" (133; bk. 2, ch. 4).

16. plays: Almost all plays are divided into acts and/or scenes. For plays that do not include line numbering throughout, cite the page number in the edition you have been using, followed by act and/or scene numbers as applicable:

- As Angie and Joyce begin drinking together Angie pronounces the occasion "better than Christmas" (72; act 3).

- Near the conclusion of Inchbald's *Wives as They Were* Bronzely declares that he has been "made to think with reverence on the matrimonial compact" (62; act 5, sc. 4).

For plays written entirely or largely in verse, where line numbers are typically provided throughout, you should omit the reference to the page number in the citation. Instead, cite the act, scene, and line numbers, using Arabic numerals. For a Shakespeare play, if the title isn't clear from the introduction to a quotation, an abbreviation of the title may also be used. The in-text citation below is for Shakespeare's *The Merchant of Venice*, Act 2, Scene 3, lines 2–4:

- Jessica clearly has some fondness for Launcelot: "Our house is hell, and thou, a merry devil, / Dost rob it of some taste of tediousness. / But fare thee well; there is a ducat for thee" (*MV* 2.3.2–4).

17. works without page numbers: If you are citing literary texts where you have consulted editions from other sources (on the web or in an ebook, for instance), the principles are exactly the same, except that you need not cite page numbers. For example, if the online Gutenberg edition of Fielding's *Joseph Andrews* were being cited, the citation would be as follows:

- When Joseph and Fanny are by themselves, they immediately express their affection for each other, or, as Fielding puts it, "solace themselves" with "amorous discourse" (ch. 26).

Students should be cautioned that online editions of literary texts are often unreliable. Typically there are far more typos and other errors in online versions of literary texts than there are in print versions, and such things as the layout of poems are also frequently incorrect. It is often possible to exercise judgment about such matters, however. If, for example, you are not required to base your essay on a particular copy of a Thomas Hardy poem but may find your own, you will be far better off using the text you will find on the Representative Poetry Online site run out of the University of Toronto than you will using a text you might find on a "World's Finest Love Poems" site.

18. sacred texts: The Bible and other sacred texts that are available in many editions should be cited in a way that enables the reader to check the reference in any edition. For the Bible, book, chapter, and verse should all be cited, using periods for separation. The reference below is to Genesis, chapter 2, verse 1.

- According to the Judeo-Christian story of creation, at the end of the sixth day "the heavens and the earth were finished" (Gen. 2.1).

19. works in an anthology or book of readings: In the in-text citation for a work in an anthology, use the name of the author of the work, not that of the editor of the anthology. The page number, however, should be that found in the anthology. The following citation refers to an article by Frederic W. Gleach in an anthology edited by Jennifer Brown and Elizabeth Vibert.

- One of the essays in Brown and Vibert's collection argues that we should rethink the Pocahontas myth (Gleach 48).

In your list of Works Cited, this work should be alphabetized under Gleach, the author of the piece you have consulted, not under Brown. If you cite another work by a different author from the same anthology or book of readings, that should appear as a separate entry in your list of Works Cited—again, alphabetized under the author's name.

20. tweets: Cite tweets by giving the author's name in your text rather than in an in-text citation.

- Stephen King has written about the elusive nature of artistic inspiration, tweeting for example in May 2021 that "[g]ood writing is a delight to those who read it and a mystery to those who write it."

O *About Works Cited*

MLA Core Elements

The Works Cited list in MLA style is an alphabetized list at the end of the essay (or article or book). The entire list, like the main part of the essay, should be double-spaced throughout, and each entry should be given a hanging indent: the first line is flush with the left-hand margin, and each subsequent line is indented one tab space.

The Works Cited list should include information about all the sources you have cited. Do not include works that you consulted but did not cite in the body of your text.

MLA style provides a set of citation guidelines that the writer follows and adapts, regardless of whether the source being cited is print, digital, audio, visual, or any other form of media. All sources share what the MLA calls "Core Elements," and these, listed in order, create the citation for each entry: Author, Title of Source, Title of Container (larger whole), Contributor, Version, Number, Publisher, Publication Date, and Location. Each element is followed by the punctuation marks shown in the table below, unless it is the last element, which should always close with a period. (There are a few exceptions to this rule, which are outlined below.) Most sources don't have all the elements (some don't have an author, for example, or a version, or a location); if you find that this is the case, omit the element and move on to the next.

The table can function as a guide when creating citations. Once you have found all the publication details for your source, place them in order and punctuate according to the table, leaving out any elements for which you don't have information. It is common for a source to have more than one "container"—such as an article printed in a journal and found on an online database. For sources like these, the table below can be filled out a second time, beginning with item 3 for the second container. Please see the section below on "Title of Container" for details and examples.

1. Author.
2. Title of source.
3. Title of container,
4. Contributor,
5. Version,
6. Number,
7. Publisher,
8. Publication date,
9. Location.

In the sections below, you will discover how to identify the core elements of MLA style and how to use them across media. For a list of examples, please see pages 67–83.

Author

This element begins your citation. For a **single author**, list the author's last name first, followed by a comma, and then the author's first name or initials (use whatever appears on the work's title page or copyright page), followed by a period.

> Graham, Jorie. *From the New World*. Ecco, 2015.

> Johnson, George M. *All Boys Aren't Blue*. Farrar, Straus and Giroux, 2020.

If a source has **two authors**, the first author's name should appear with the last name first, followed by a comma and *and*. Note also that the authors' names should appear in the order they are listed; sometimes this is not alphabetical.

> Rectenwald, Michael, and Lisa Carl. *Academic Writing, Real World Topics*. Broadview Press, 2015.

MLA Style

If there are **three or more authors**, include only the first author's name, reversed, followed by a comma and *et al.* (the abbreviation of the Latin *et alia*, meaning *and others*).

> Waldron, Janice L., et al. *The Oxford Handbook of Social Media and Music Learning*. Oxford UP, 2020.

Sources that are **edited** rather than authored are usually cited in a similar way; add "editor" or "editors" after the name(s) and before the title.

> Renker, Elizabeth, editor. *Poems: A Concise Anthology*. Broadview Press, 2016.

When referring to an edited version of a work written by another author or authors, list the editor(s) after the title, in the Contributor element.

> Trollope, Anthony. *The Eustace Diamonds*. 1873. Edited by Stephen Gill and John Sutherland, Penguin, 1986.

Authors can be organizations, institutions, associations, or government agencies ("corporate authors"). If a work has been issued by a **corporate author** and no author is identified, the entry should be listed by the name of the organization that produced it, using the name of the organization as recorded by the source.

> Ontario, Ministry of Natural Resources. *Achieving Balance: Ontario's Long-Term Energy Plan*. Queen's Printer for Ontario, 2016, www.energy. gov.on.ca/en/ltep/achieving-balance-ontarios-long -term-energy-plan. Accessed 10 June 2021.

If the work is published by the same organization that is the corporate author, skip the author element and list only the publisher. The citation will begin with the source title.

2020 Annual Report. Broadview Press, 2021.

"History of the Arms and Great Seal of the Commonwealth of Massachusetts." Commonwealth of Massachusetts, www.sec/state.ma.us/pre/presea/sealhis/htm. Accessed 5 May 2021.

"Our Mandate." Art Gallery of Ontario, www.ago.net/mandate. Accessed 10 May 2021.

Works with an **anonymous author** should be alphabetized by title, omitting the author element.

Sir Gawain and the Green Knight. Edited by Paul Battles, Broadview Press, 2012.

Works under a **pseudonym**, or **works that are by an author that has published under more than one name**, can be treated in several ways. The pseudonym or name that your source records as author may simply be used as-is in the author element. If you are citing an older work by someone who has since changed their name, you may substitute in the current name the person is using. For trans authors, for example, use an author's chosen name—do not mention former names in either your citations or your prose, regardless of the name that is listed by your source. MLA calls this "consolidating"—this way, all works by one person can be cited under one name. For example, if you are citing the novelist Agatha Christie (who also wrote under the name Mary Westmacott), it is fine to consolidate the titles under "Agatha Christie" (unless the pseudonym is relevant to your writing, in which case see other options below):

Christie, Agatha. *Absent in the Spring*. 1944. HarperCollins, 1997.

---. *Murder on the Orient Express*. 1934. HarperCollins, 2011.

If a writer uses more than one pseudonym, it may be useful to cite their works using the writer's better-known name. In this case, you may use the better-known name in the author element, followed by the lesser-known name in square brackets and preceded by *published as* (in italics).

> Oates, Joyce Carol [*published as* Lauren Kelly]. *Take Me, Take Me with You*. HarperCollins, 2005.

You may also simply place the author's more well-known name in square brackets and omit the lesser-known pseudonym, indicating that the name has been supplied by you and was originally published under another name.

> [Oates, Joyce Carol]. *Take Me, Take Me with You*. HarperCollins, 2005.

Online usernames are copied out exactly as they appear on the screen.

> @newyorker. "With the resignation of Turkey's Prime Minister, the country's President now stands alone and unchallenged." *Twitter*, 6 May 2016, www.twitter.com/NewYorker/status/728676985254379520.

Note that the author element is flexible. If you are discussing the work of a film director, for example, the director's name should be placed in the author element, with a descriptor.

> Hitchcock, Alfred, director. *The Lady Vanishes*. United Artists, 1938.

If, on the other hand, you are discussing film editing, you would place the film editor in the author element. In this case, you might also include Hitchcock's name in the "Contributor" element.

> Dearing, R.E., film editor. *The Lady Vanishes*. Directed by Alfred Hitchcock, United Artists, 1938.

If no single contributor's work is of particular importance in your discussion of a film or television source, omit the author element altogether.

> "The Buys." *The Wire*, created by David Simon and Ed Burns, directed by Peter Medak, season 1, episode 3, HBO, 16 June 2002.

If you are citing a **translated source** and the translation itself is the focus of your work, the translator or translators can be placed in the author element.

> Lodge, Kirsten, translator. *Notes from the Underground.* By Fyodor Dostoevsky, edited by Kirsten Lodge, Broadview Press, 2014.

When the work itself is the focus, as is usually the case, the author should remain in the author element, and the translator moved to the "Contributor" element:

> Dostoevsky, Fyodor. *Notes from the Underground.* Translated and edited by Kirsten Lodge, Broadview Press, 2014.

This principle holds true across media and elements. Adapt the MLA structure to create citations that are clear, relevant to your work, and useful to your reader.

Title of Source

The title of your source follows the author element. Copy the title as you find it in the source, but with MLA-standard capitalization and punctuation. Capitalize the first word, the last word, and all key words, but not articles, prepositions, coordinating conjunctions, or the *to* in infinitives.

> Carson, Anne. *The Albertine Workout.* New Directions, 2014.

If there is a **subtitle**, include it after the main title, following a colon.

> Bök, Christian. *The Xenotext: Book 1*. Coach House Books, 2015.

Your title gives the reader information about the source. Italicized titles indicate that the source is a complete, independent whole. A title enclosed in quotation marks tells the reader that the source is part of a larger work.

A **book** is an independent whole, so the title is italicized.

> Sowerby, Githa. *Three Plays*. Edited by J. Ellen Gainor, Broadview Press, 2021.

Other examples include **long poems** (*In Memoriam*), **magazines** (*The New Yorker*), **newspapers** (*The Guardian*), **journals** (*The American Poetry Review*), **websites** (*The Camelot Project*), **films** (*Memento*), **television shows** (*The X-Files*), and **compact discs** or **record albums** (*Dark Side of the Moon*).

A **poem**, **short story**, or **essay** within a larger collection is placed in quotation marks.

> Wordsworth, William. "The Solitary Reaper." *Poems, in Two Volumes*, edited by Richard Matlak, Broadview Press, 2016, p. 153.

Other examples include **chapters in books** ("The Autist Artist" in *The Man Who Mistook His Wife for a Hat and Other Clinical Tales*), **encyclopedia articles** ("Existentialism"), **essays in books or journals** ("Salvation in the Garden: Daoism and Ecology" in *Daoism and Ecology: Ways within a Cosmic Landscape*), **short stories** ("Young Goodman Brown"), **short poems** ("Daddy"), **pages on websites**

("The Fisher King" from *The Camelot Project*), **episodes of television shows** ("Small Potatoes" from *The X-Files*), and **songs** ("Eclipse" from *Dark Side of the Moon*). Put the titles of **public lectures** in quotation marks as well ("Walls in *The Epic of Gilgamesh*").

These formatting rules apply across media forms. A website is placed in italics; a posting on the website is placed in quotation marks.

> Stein, Sadie. "Casting the Runes." *The Daily: The Paris Review Blog*, 9 Oct. 2015, www.theparisreview.org/ blog/2015/10/09/casting-the-runes/.

If the title of a stand-alone work contains the title of a work that is not independent, the latter is put in double quotation marks, and the entire title is put in italics (*"Self-Reliance" and Other Essays*). If the title of a stand-alone work appears within the title of another independent work, MLA recommends that the latter be put in italics and the former not (*Chaucer's* House of Fame: *The Poetics of Skeptical Fideism*). If the title of a non-independent work is embedded in another title of the same kind, put the inner title in single quotation marks and the outer title in double quotation marks ("The Drama of Donne's 'The Indifferent'").

When a stand-alone work appears in a **collection**, the work's title remains in italics.

> James, Henry. *The American. Henry James: Novels 1871–1880*, edited by William T. Stafford, Library of America, 1983.

Title of Container

Very often your source is found within a larger context, such as an **anthology**, **periodical**, **newspaper**, **digital platform**, or **website**. When this is the case, the larger whole is called the "container." For an article in a newspaper, for example, the article is the "source" and the newspaper is the "container." For a song on an **album**, the song is the "source" and the album is the "container."

The title of the container is usually italicized and followed by a comma.

> Russell, Anna. "The Beguiling Legacy of *Alice in Wonderland*." *The New Yorker*, 11 July 2021, www.newyorker.com/culture/culture-desk/ the-beguiling-legacy-of-alice-in-wonderland.

The container is anything that contains another work: a website; a book that is a collection of stories, poems, plays, or essays; a magazine; a journal; an album; or a database.

When doing research, particularly online, one often comes across nested containers, in which, for example, an article is found in a periodical, which is itself found on a database. All containers are recorded in the citation, so your reader knows exactly how to find your source. Add more container elements as needed. Additional containers should follow the period at the end of the information given for the first container (usually after the date or location element).

It can be helpful to see this process charted out. Notice that the publication information for the containers follows that of the source.

Here is an example of an **article from a periodical**, accessed from an online database.

1. Author.	Lamothe, Daphne.
2. Title of source.	"The City-Child's Quest: Spatiality and Sociality in Paule Marshall's *The Fisher King*."
CONTAINER 1:	
3. Title of container,	*Meridians,*
4. Contributor,	
5. Version,	
6. Number,	vol. 15, no. 2,
7. Publisher,	
8. Publication date,	2017,
9. Location.	pp. 491–506.
CONTAINER 2:	
3. Title of container,	*JSTOR,*
4. Contributor,	
5. Version,	
6. Number,	
7. Publisher,	
8. Publication date,	
9. Location.	www.jstor.org/stable/10.2979/meridians.15.2.10.
10. Supplemental Element.	Accessed 13 July 2021.

MLA Style

Citation as It Would Appear in the Works Cited List:

> Lamothe, Daphne. "The City-Child's Quest: Spatial-
> ity and Sociality in Paule Marshall's *The Fisher
> King*." *Meridians*, vol. 15, no. 2, 2017, pp.
> 491–506. *JSTOR*, www.jstor.org/stable/10.2979/
> meridians.15.2.10. Accessed 13 July 2021.

The next example is an **e-book** accessed from a digital platform.

1. Author.	Copeland, Edward, and Juliet McMaster, editors.
2. Title of source.	*The Cambridge Companion to Jane Austen.*
CONTAINER 1:	
3. Title of container,	
4. Contributor,	
5. Version,	2nd ed.,
6. Number,	
7. Publisher,	Cambridge UP,
8. Publication date,	2010.
9. Location.	
CONTAINER 2:	
3. Title of container,	*Cambridge Core,*
4. Contributor,	
5. Version,	
6. Number,	

7. Publisher,	
8. Publication date,	2011,
9. Location.	https://doi.org/10.1017/ CCO9780521763080.

Citation as It Would Appear in the Works Cited List:

Copeland, Edward, and Juliet McMaster, editors. *The Cambridge Companion to Jane Austen*. 2nd ed., Cambridge UP, 2010. *Cambridge Core*, 2011, https://doi.org/10.1017/CCO9780521763080.

The elements are recorded sequentially to create your citation. Notice that any elements that don't apply to this source are left out. Note that for a **self-contained e-book** that you access on an e-reader or in a proprietary web app, you may treat the citation as you would a print book, adding "e-book ed." in the Version element.

1. Author.	Austen, Jane.
2. Title of source.	*Pride and Prejudice.*
CONTAINER 1:	
3. Title of container,	
4. Contributor,	Edited by Robert P. Irvine,
5. Version,	2nd ed., e-book ed.,
6. Number,	
7. Publisher,	Broadview Press,
8. Publication date,	2020.
9. Location.	

Citation as It Would Appear in the Works Cited List:

> Austen, Jane. *Pride and Prejudice*. Edited by Robert P.
>   Irvine, 2nd ed., e-book ed., Broadview Press, 2020.

Here is an example citation of a **performance in a television series**, accessed on Hulu.

1. Author.	Washington, Kerry, performer.
2. Title of source.	"The Spark."
CONTAINER 1:	
3. Title of container,	*Little Fires Everywhere*,
4. Contributor,	directed by Lynn Shelton,
5. Version,	
6. Number,	season 1, episode 1,
7. Publisher,	Best Day Ever Productions et al.,
8. Publication date,	2020.
9. Location.	
CONTAINER 2:	
3. Title of container,	*Hulu*,
4. Contributor,	
5. Version,	
6. Number,	
7. Publisher,	
8. Publication date,	
9. Location.	www.hulu.com/series/little-fires -everywhere-bce24897-1a74-48a3 -95e8-6cdd530dde4c.

Citation as It Would Appear in the Works Cited List:

Washington, Kerry, performer. "The Spark." *Little Fires Everywhere*, directed by Lynn Shelton, season 1, episode 1, Best Day Ever Productions et al., 2020. *Hulu*, www.hulu.com/series/little-fires-everywhere -bce24897-1a74-48a3-95e8-6cdd530dde4c.

Contributor

There may be other key people who should be credited in your citation as contributors. This element follows the title of the source and the container (if there is one). The MLA recommends that you include the names of contributors who are important to your research, or if they help your reader to identify the source. Before each name, place a description of the role (do not abbreviate):

adapted by	introduction by
directed by	narrated by
edited by	performance by
illustrated by	translated by

If your listing of a contributor follows the source title, it is capitalized (following a period). If the contributor follows a container, it will be lower-case (following a comma).

Mechain, Gwerful. *The Works of Gwerful Mechain*. Translated by Katie Gramich, Broadview Press, 2018.

James, Henry. *The American. Henry James: Novels 1871–1880*, edited by William T. Stafford, Library of America, 1983.

In the Contributor element, include the most relevant contributors not already mentioned in the author element. If you are writing about a television episode and a certain performance is one of the elements you discuss, for example, include the performer's name in the Contributor element, along with any other contributors you wish to include.

> Medak, Peter, director. "The Buys." *The Wire*, created by David Simon and Ed Burns, performance by Dominic West, season 1, episode 3, HBO, 16 June 2002.

Note that the MLA guidelines are flexible; for this part of the citation especially, consider what your readers most need to know about your source and include that information. Note also that there is some flexibility in the author element; if a particular performance or other contribution is the major focus in your discussion of the source, it can be cited in the author element instead.

Version

If your source is **one of several editions**, an **e-book edition**, or a **revised version**, record those details in this element of your citation, followed by a comma. The word "edition" is abbreviated in your citation (ed.).

> Edgeworth, Maria, et al. *Moral Tales: A Selection*. Edited by Robin Runia, e-book ed., Broadview Press, 2021.

> Fowles, John. *The Magus*. Rev. ed., Jonathan Cape, 1977.

> Shelley, Mary. *Frankenstein*. Edited by D.L. Macdonald and Kathleen Scherf, 3rd ed., Broadview Press, 2012.

You may also come across **expanded editions**, **revised editions**, and **updated editions**, all of which may be noted in this element of your citation. Different media might use different terminology. For example in film you may find a

director's cut, or in music an **abridged version** of a concerto: use the same principles as above, providing the relevant information in the Version element of your citation.

> Coen, Ethan, and Joel Coen, directors. *Blood Simple.* Director's cut, Universal, 2001.

Number

If your source is part of a **multi-volume work**, or if it is part of a journal that is issued in numbers and/or volumes, include the volume information in this Number element of your citation.

If you are citing **two or more volumes** of a multi-volume work, the entry may note the total number of volumes. If you cite only one of the volumes, list it after the title.

> Jeeves, Julie, editor. *A Reference Guide to Spanish Architecture.* 3 vols., Hackett, 2005.

> Mercer, Bobby, editor. *A Reference Guide to French Architecture.* Vol. 1, Hackett, 2002.

Include the **volume and issue numbers** for journals. Use the abbreviations *vol.* for volume and *no.* for issue number.

> Gregory, Elizabeth. "Marianne Moore's 'Blue Bug': A Dialogic Ode on Celebrity, Race, Gender, and Age." *Modernism/Modernity*, vol. 22, no. 4, 2015, pp. 759–86.

Some journals do not use volume numbers and give only an issue number.

> Sanger, Richard. "Goodbye, Seamus." *Brick*, no. 93, summer 2014, pp. 153–57.

MLA Style

The Number element is also where you record issue numbers for comic books, or the season and episode numbers for a television series.

> Washington, Kerry, performer. "The Spark." *Little Fires Everywhere*, directed by Lynn Shelton, season 1, episode 1, Best Day Ever Productions et al., 2020. *Hulu*, www.hulu.com/series/little-fires-everywhere-bce24897-1a74-48a3-95e8-6cdd530dde4c.

Publisher

In this element of your citation, record the organization that produced the source, whether it be the publisher of a book, the organization running a website, or the studio producing a film. (In the case of a secondary container, include the organization that produced the container.) Do not abbreviate, except in the case of university presses, which may be abbreviated as *UP*.

To find the publisher of a **book**, look on the title page or on the copyright page.

> Joyce, James. *Exiles*. Edited by Keri Walsh, Oxford UP, 2021.

> Rush, Rebecca. *Kelroy*. Edited by Betsy Klimasmith, Broadview Press, 2016.

For a **film** or **television series**, the studio or company that produced the show is recorded in the information on the back of a DVD or in the opening and closing credits.

> Simon, David, creator. *The Wire*. HBO, 2002–2008.

For **websites**, the publisher's information can often be found in the copyright notice at the bottom of the page.

Bogan, Louise. "Women." 1922. *Representative Poetry Online*, edited by Ian Lancashire, University of Toronto, 2000.

You may omit a publisher's name in the following kinds of publications:

- A periodical (journal, magazine, newspaper).
- A work published by its author or editor.
- A website whose title is essentially the same as the name of the publisher.
- A website not involved in producing the works it is making available (YouTube, JSTOR, ProQuest). These are listed as containers, but not as publishers.

If **two or more publishers** are listed for your source, cite them both and separate them with a forward slash (/).

Banting, Keith G., editor. *Thinking Outside the Box: Innovation in Policy Ideas*. School of Policy Studies, Queen's University / McGill–Queen's University Press, 2015.

Publication Date

In this element of your citation, record the date of publication for your source. For **books**, this date is found on the copyright page (and sometimes on the title page). If several editions are listed, use the date for the edition you have consulted.

Stevenson, Robert Louis. *Strange Case of Dr. Jekyll and Mr. Hyde*. Edited by Martin A. Danahay, 3rd ed., Broadview Press, 2015.

Online sources almost always have a date posted, and this is the date you should record in this element.

Heller, Nathan. "The Big Uneasy: What's Roiling the
    Liberal-Arts Campus?" *The New Yorker*, 30 May
    2016, www.newyorker.com/magazine/2016/05/30/
    the-new-activism-of-liberal-arts-colleges.

A source may be associated with **more than one publication date**. An article online may have been previously
published in print, or an article printed in a book may
have been published previously in a periodical. In this
case, the MLA recommends that you record the date that
is most relevant to your use of the source. If you consulted
the online version of an article, for example, ignore the
date of print publication and cite the online publication
date.

For books, we record the year of publication. For other
sources, whether to include a year, month, and day depends
on your source and the context in which you are using it.
If you are citing an **episode from a television series**, for
example, it is usually enough to record the year it aired.

Medak, Peter, director. "The Buys." *The Wire*, created
    by David Simon and Ed Burns, season 1, episode
    3, HBO, 2002.

If, however, the context surrounding the episode is being
discussed in your work, you should be more specific about
the date:

Medak, Peter, director. "The Buys." *The Wire*, created by
    David Simon and Ed Burns, season 1, episode 3,
    HBO, 16 June 2002.

For a **video posted on a website**, include the date on which
the video was posted. In the example below, the posting date
should be included in the second container, which records

MLA Style

the details for the digital platform. The date the video was released is included in the publication details for the source.

> McDonald, Emily, director. *Looking Back with Pride.* Forever Pictures, 2021. *Vimeo*, uploaded by Emily McDonald, 21 June 2021, www.vimeo. com/565585933.

If you are citing a **comment posted on a web page**, and the time the content was posted is indicated, include the time in your entry.

> Evan. Comment on "Another Impasse on Gun Bills, Another Win for Hyperpolitics." *The New York Times*, 21 June 2016, 9:02 a.m., www.nytimes. com/2016/06/22/us/politics/washington-congress -gun-control.html.

Larger projects are created over a longer span of time. If you are documenting a web project as a whole, include the full range of years during which it was developed.

> Secord, James A., et al., editors. *Darwin Correspondence Project.* 1974–2016, www.darwinproject.ac.uk/.

The dates of publication for **periodicals** vary. Include in full the information provided by the copyright page, whether it be indicated by season, year, month, week, or day.

> Gander, Forrest. "A Most Ingenious Work of Literature." *Brick*, no. 107, summer 2021, pp. 11–18.

> Salenius, Sirpa. "Transatlantic Interracial Sisterhoods: Sarah Remond, Ellen Craft, and Harriet Jacobs in England." *Frontiers: A Journal of Women Studies*, vol. 38, no. 1, 2017, pp. 166–96. *JSTOR*, www.jstor. org/stable/10.5250/fronjwomestud.38.1.0166.

MLA Style

Location

The content of the Location element varies considerably between print, digital, and other sources.

For **print sources** within a periodical or anthology, record a page number (preceded by p.) or a range of page numbers (preceded by pp.).

> Gregory, Elizabeth. "Marianne Moore's 'Blue Bug': A Dialogic Ode on Celebrity, Race, Gender, and Age." *Modernism/Modernity*, vol. 22, no. 4, 2015, pp. 759–86.

An **online work** is located by its DOI or URL. If a DOI (Digital Object Identifier) is available, it is a more reliable and preferred option, as DOIs do not change when the source moves (whereas URLs do). If your source has no DOI but offers a "stable" URL, choose that one to include in your citation. The publisher in this case has agreed not to change the URL. Note that the MLA considers the inclusion of URLs to be optional, as there are downsides to including them (such as their instability and their tendency to create messier citations). In general, however, it is best to include them, unless your instructor advises otherwise. When copying a URL into your citation, remove the *http://*; this means that usually the URL will begin with *www*. MLA recommends truncating excessively long URLs, leaving readers enough of the address to find the source but avoiding an unruly citation. If you need to break a URL or DOI over two or more lines, do not insert any hyphens at the break point; instead, when possible, break after a colon or slash or before other marks of punctuation.

MLA Style

Jesse, Tom. "John Ashbery's Unexceptional Politics." *Pacific Coast Philology*, vol. 55, no. 2, 2021, pp. 171–90. *JSTOR*, www.jstor.org/stable/10.5325/pacicoasphil.55.2.0171.

Yearling, R. "*Hamlet* and the Limits of Narrative." *Essays in Criticism: A Quarterly Journal of Literary Criticism*, vol. 65, no. 4, 2015, pp. 368–82. *ProQuest*, https://doi.org/10.1093/escrit/cgv022.

We find a **television episode** on a DVD by its disc number. Place the disc number in the Location element.

"The Buys." *The Wire*, created by David Simon and Ed Burns, directed by Peter Medak, season 1, episode 3, HBO, 2002, disc 1.

For a **work of art** that you have seen in person, cite the name of the institution and city where you saw it in the Location element. Leave out the name of the city if the city name is part of the institution name (e.g., The Art Institute of Chicago).

Sargent, John Singer. *Henry James*. 1913, National Portrait Gallery, London.

Some **archived sources** have a different system for locating objects in the archive. Where this is the case, include the code or number in the Location element.

Blake, William. *The Marriage of Heaven and Hell*. 1790–1793, The Fitzwilliam Museum, Cambridge, 123-1950. Illuminated printed book.

If you are citing a **live performance** or **lecture**, name the location and the city. Omit the city name if it is part of the location name.

MLA Style

Royal Winnipeg Ballet. *The Princess and the Goblin.* Directed and choreographed by Twyla Tharp, performances by Paloma Herrera and Dmitri Dovgoselets, 17 Oct. 2012, Centennial Concert Hall, Winnipeg.

Supplemental Elements

You may include any of the following elements in your citation if you think they are necessary or helpful to your reader. Supplemental elements are typically inserted into two possible places in your citation—after the title of your source, if it applies primarily to the source (such as an original publication date), or at the end of the citation, if it applies to the citation as a whole (such as a date of access). Add a period at the end of a supplemental element, regardless of its placement.

Date of Original Publication

If your source has been republished, you may give your reader some important context if you include the date of original publication. If you do so, place the date immediately after the source title and close with a period.

Trollope, Anthony. *The Eustace Diamonds.* 1873. Edited by Stephen Gill and John Sutherland, Penguin, 1986.

City of Publication

Including the city of publication is not very useful these days, so the MLA has decided to remove this element from citations. There are two situations, however, where you may wish to include the city. If the book was published before 1900, the city of publication is associated more closely with the source than the publisher. For these books, you may substitute the city of publication for the publisher.

> Dickens, Charles. *Our Mutual Friend*. Vol. 1, New York, 1865.

Some publishers release more than one version of a text in different countries (a British and an American edition, for example). If you are reading an unexpected version of a text, or the version you are reading has historical significance, place the name of the city in front of the publisher.

> Lawrence, D.H. *Lady Chatterley's Lover*. London, Penguin, 1960.

Books in a Series
If your source is a book in a series, you may add the series name in roman (i.e., without italics) at the end of your citation, preceded by a period.

> Klooster, Wim, editor. *Spanish American Independence Movements: A History in Documents*. Broadview Press, 2021. Broadview Sources Series.

Unexpected Type of Work
If your source needs further explanation, place a descriptive term (e-mail, transcript, broadcast, street performance, talk, address) at the end of the citation, preceded by a period.

> Rosenheim, Jeff. "Diane Arbus." Art Gallery of Ontario, 6 May 2016, Toronto. Lecture.

Date of Access
It is optional to include a date of access for your online citations, but it can be a good idea, particularly if the source does not have a date of publication.

Crawford, Isabella Valancy. "The Canoe." *Representative Poetry Online*, edited by Ian Lancashire, University of Toronto, www.tspace.library.utoronto.ca/html/1807/4350/poem596.html. Accessed 10 Dec. 2020.

Examples

The following are examples of MLA-style citations for sources across various media. While these examples can offer useful guidance, remember that the MLA guidelines may be adapted to suit the details of the sources you are documenting, as well as the context in which you are using them.

21. single author:

Graham, Jorie. *From the New World*. Ecco, 2015.

Ingalls, Rachel. *Mrs Caliban*. 1982. Faber & Faber, 2021.

22. two authors:

Davis, Lydia, and Eliot Weinberger. *Two American Scenes*. New Directions, 2013. Pamphlets Series.

Rectenwald, Michael, and Lisa Carl. *Academic Writing, Real World Topics*. Broadview Press, 2015.

23. three or more authors:

Fantuzzi, Marco, et al., editors. *Reception in the Greco-Roman World: Literary Studies in Theory and Practice*. Cambridge UP, 2021.

Fromkin, Victoria, et al. *An Introduction to Language*. 4th Canadian ed., Nelson, 2010.

MLA Style

24. corporate author:

> *2020 Annual Report.* Broadview Press, 2021.

> "History of the Arms and Great Seal of the Common-
> wealth of Massachusetts." Commonwealth of Mas-
> sachusetts, www.sec/state.ma.us/pre/presea/sealhis/
> htm. Accessed 15 June 2021.

> Ontario, Ministry of Natural Resources. *Achieving Bal-
> ance: Ontario's Long-Term Energy Plan.* Queen's
> Printer for Ontario, 2016, www.energy.gov.on.ca/
> en/ltep/achieving-balance-ontarios-long-term
> -energy-plan. Accessed 10 May 2021.

25. works with an anonymous author: Works with an
anonymous author should be alphabetized by title.

> *Pearl.* Edited and translated by Jane Beal, Broadview
> Press, 2020.

26. two or more works by the same author: The author's
name should appear for the first entry only; for subsequent
entries substitute three hyphens for the name of the author.

> Menand, Louis. "Bad Comma: Lynne Truss's Strange
> Grammar." Review of *Eats, Shoots and Leaves*,
> by Lynne Truss. *The New Yorker,* 28 June 2004,
> www.newyorker.com/magazine/2004/06/28/bad
> -comma. Accessed 10 Feb. 2021.

> ---. *The Metaphysical Club: A Story of Ideas in America.*
> Farrar, Straus and Giroux, 2001.

27. works under a pseudonym: These are given using the
same formatting as author's names. Online usernames are
given as they appear.

@TheAtlantic. "The president is loath to acknowledge that many Americans support the recent
attacks on democracy, 'and those who don't face
a system stacked against them,' @GrahamDavidA
writes." *Twitter*, 14 July 2021, www.twitter.com/
TheAtlantic/status/1415363709950701572.

28. edited works:

Renker, Elizabeth, editor. *Poems: A Concise Anthology*.
Broadview Press, 2016.

When referring to an edited version of a work written by
another author or authors, list the editor(s) after the title.

Trollope, Anthony. *The Eustace Diamonds*. 1873. Edited
by Stephen Gill and John Sutherland, Penguin,
1986.

29. works in translation: The translator is normally listed
in the Contributor element of the citation.

Bolaño, Roberto. *By Night in Chile*. Translated by Chris
Andrews, New Directions, 2003.

If your work focuses on the translation itself, you may list
the translator in the author element, moving the author to
the Contributor element.

Andrews, Chris, translator. *By Night in Chile*. By Roberto
Bolaño, New Directions, 2003.

30. selections from anthologies or collections of readings:
A selection from a collection of readings or an anthology
should begin with the name of the author of the selection.
If they are available, be sure to add the selection's inclusive
page numbers after the anthology's publication date.

Crawford, Isabella Valancy. "The Canoe." *Representative Poetry Online*, edited by Ian Lancashire, University of Toronto, 1997, www.rpo.library.utoronto.ca/poems/canoe. Accessed 7 July 2021.

Skelton, John. *Magnificence. The Broadview Anthology of Tudor Drama*, edited by Alan Stewart, Broadview Press, 2021, pp. 125–80.

Whitman, Walt. "Song of the Redwood-Tree." *Leaves of Grass*, Boston: James R Osgood and Co, 1881–82. *The Walt Whitman Archive*, edited by Matt Cohen et al., www.whitmanarchive.org/published/LG/1891/poems/93.

31. cross-references for works from the same collection or anthology: It can be more efficient to create a full entry for the collection or anthology, and then to list each cited item in its own entry. Position the entries in the Works Cited list alphabetically, as you normally would, and use a short form for the collection or anthology, as in the following example:

Brown, Jennifer S.H., and Elizabeth Vibert, editors. *Reading Beyond Words: Contexts for Native History*. Broadview Press, 1996.

Cruikshank, Julie. "Discovery of Gold on the Klondike: Perspectives from Oral Tradition." Brown and Vibert, pp. 433–59.

Gleach, Frederic W. "Controlled Speculation: Interpreting the Saga of Pocahontas and Captain John Smith." Brown and Vibert, pp. 21–42.

32. multi-volume works: If you are citing one or more of the volumes, list them after the title. The entry may note the total number of volumes at the end of the citation (this is optional).

> Jeeves, Julie, editor. *A Reference Guide to Spanish Archi-tecture.* 3 vols., Hackett, 2005.

> Mercer, Bobby, editor. *A Reference Guide to French Archi-tecture.* Vol. 1, Hackett, 2002. 3 vols.

33. different editions: The edition should be specified whenever it is not the first edition. Include whatever the title page indicates about the particular edition, and use abbreviations (e.g., *rev. ed.* for *revised edition*, *2nd ed.* for *second edition*, and so on).

> Acheson, Katherine O. *Writing Essays about Literature: A Guide for University and College Students.* 2nd ed., Broadview Press, 2021.

> Fowles, John. *The Magus.* Rev. ed., Jonathan Cape, 1977.

> *The Bible.* Authorized King James Version, Oxford UP, 2008.

34. republished sources: When a source was previously published in a different form, you may include information about the prior publication. This is a supplemental element; include this information at your discretion, if you feel it would give your reader important context for the source.

> MacMillan, Margaret. "Hubris." *History's People: Person-alities and the Past,* Massey Lectures, CBC Radio, 3 Nov. 2015, www.cbc.ca/radio/ideas/history-s -people-personalities-the-past-lecture-2-1.3301571. Podcast. Originally delivered at the Arts and Cul-ture Centre, St. John's, NL, 25 Sept. 2015, 7:00 p.m. Lecture.

35. reference work entries: List by the author of the entry, if known; otherwise, list by the entry itself. The citation of a well-known reference work (because such works are frequently updated) should not have full publication details; provide the edition number, date, and location only. Don't include page numbers for works that arrange their entries alphabetically.

> "Artificial." *Oxford English Dictionary.* 2nd ed., 1989.

> "Baldwin, James, 1924–1987." *ProQuest Biographies*, 2006. *Literature Online*, www-proquest -com./encyclopedias-reference-works/baldwin -james-1924-1987. Accessed 15 July 2021.

> Fowler, H.W. "Unique." *The King's English*, 2nd ed., 1908. *Bartleby.com*, www.bartleby.com/116/108. html#2. Accessed 20 May 2021.

36. works with a title in the title: A title that is usually italicized should remain italicized when it appears within quotation marks:

> Yearling, R. "*Hamlet* and the Limits of Narrative." *Essays in Criticism: A Quarterly Journal of Literary Criticism,* vol. 65, no. 4, 2015, pp. 368–82. *ProQuest*, https://doi.org/10.1093/escrit/cgv022.

Titles that are in quotation marks that appear within other titles in quotation marks are enclosed by single quotation marks:

> Berndt, Katrin. "Trapped in Class? Material Manifestations of Poverty and Prosperity in Alice Munro's 'Royal Beatings' and 'The Beggar Maid.'" *Neohelicon*, vol. 47, 18 Aug. 2020, pp. 521–35. *SpringerLink Journals*, https://doi.org/10.1007/s11059-020-00550-1.

An italicized title that is included within another italicized title is neither italicized nor placed in quotation marks. It appears in roman:

> Morelli, Stefan. *Stoppard's* Arcadia *and Modern Drama.* Ashgate, 2004.

If a title normally enclosed in quotation marks appears in an italicized title, keep the quotation marks:

> Runzo, Sandra. *"Theatricals of Day": Emily Dickinson and Nineteenth-Century American Popular Culture.* U of Massachusetts P, 2019.

37. material from prefaces, introductions, etc.: If you refer to something from a work's preface, introduction, or foreword, the reference under Works Cited should begin with the name of the author of that preface, introduction, or foreword. Add inclusive page numbers after the date of publication.

> Stage, Kelly. Introduction. *The Roaring Girl*, by Thomas Middleton and Thomas Dekker, Broadview Press, 2019, pp. 7–17.

38. magazine articles: The title of the article should appear in quotation marks, the title of the magazine in italics. If no author is identified, the title of the article should appear first. If the magazine is published monthly or every two months, give the date as month and year. For magazines published weekly or every two weeks, give the date as day, month, and year. Abbreviate the names of months (except for *May, June,* and *July*).

> Enright, Robert. "Ways of Looking, Ways of Not Seeing: An Interview with Shaan Syed." *Border Crossings*, no. 156, May 2021, www.bordercrossingsmag.com/ article/ways-of-looking-ways-of-not-seeing.

"Greens in Pinstriped Suits." *The Economist*, 21 May 2016,
www.economist.com/news/business/21699141
-climate-conscious-shareholders-are-putting-big
-oil-spot-greens-pinstriped-suits.

If you accessed the article online, you may include the date
of access, though it is a supplemental element. If the website
is hosted by a body other than the magazine itself, include
it as a second container with its accompanying publication
details.

Gladwell, Malcolm. "The Art of Failure: Why Some
People Choke and Others Panic." *The New
Yorker*, 21 Aug. 2000, www.newyorker.com/
magazine/2000/08/21/the-art-of-failure. Accessed
10 Feb. 2021.

Kreimer, Julian. "Mernet Larsen." *Art in America*, vol.
104, no. 4, 2016, pp. 115–16. *Academic Search
Complete*, www.search.ebscohost.com/login
.aspx?direct=true&db=114088897&site=ehost
-live. Accessed 9 Feb. 2021.

39. newspaper articles: The basic principles to follow with
newspaper articles or editorials are the same as with magazine articles (see above). Note, however, that when the newspaper's sections are paginated separately, section as well as
page numbers are often required. If an article is not printed
on consecutive pages, include only the first page number
followed by a plus sign. In the following reference the article
begins on page 3 of the first section:

Yakabuski, Konrad. "Many Looking for Meaning in
Vice-Presidential Debate." *The Globe and Mail*, 12
Oct. 2012, p. A3+.

If you are citing an online version of a newspaper article you should include the date you accessed the site. The site name, if it is different from the container title, should also be included.

> Friedman, Lisa. "Democrats Call for a Tax on Imports from Polluting Countries." *The New York Times*, 14 July 2021, www.nytimes.com/2021/07/14/climate/border-carbon-tax-united-states.html. Accessed 2 May 2021.

40. journal articles: The basic principles are the same as with magazine articles, but entries for journal articles include the volume and issue numbers.

> Belcourt, Billy-Ray. "Meditations on Reserve Life, Bio-sociality, and the Taste of Non-Sovereignty." *Settler Colonial Studies*, vol. 8, no. 1, Jan. 2018, pp. 1–15, https://doi.org/10.1080/2201473X.2017.1279830.

If you are citing an online version of a journal article you should include any additional containers and their publication details (databases, for example).

> Sohmer, Steve. "12 June 1599: Opening Day at Shakespeare's Globe." *Early Modern Literary Studies: A Journal of Sixteenth- and Seventeenth-Century English Literature*, vol. 3, no. 1, 1997. *ProQuest,* www.extra.shu.ac.uk/emls/emlshome.html. Accessed 5 May 2021.

41. book reviews: The name of the reviewer (if it has been provided) should come first, followed by the title of the review (if there is one), and then by the information on the book itself.

Leiter, Brian, and Michael Weisberg. "Do You Only Have a Brain? On Thomas Nagel." Review of *Why the Materialist Neo-Darwinian Conception of Nature Is Almost Certainly False*, by Thomas Nagel, *The Nation,* 22 Oct. 2012, www.thenation.com/article/do-you-only-have-brain-thomas-nagel/. Accessed 20 Oct. 2021.

Lennon, J. Robert. "I Was Trying to Find the Edge." Review of *Second Place*, by Rachel Cusk, *London Review of Books*, vol. 43, no. 11, 3 June 2021, www.lrb.co.uk/the-paper/v43/n11/j.-robert-lennon/i-was-trying-to-find-the-edge.

42. periodical publications in online databases:

Moy, Olivia Loksing. "Reading in the Aftermath: An Asian American *Jane Eyre*." *Victorian Studies*, vol. 62 no. 3, 2020, pp. 406–20. *Project MUSE*, muse.jhu.edu/article/771238.

43. illustrated books: Include the illustrator's name as well as the author's name.

Juster, Norman. *The Phantom Tollbooth*. Illustrated by Jules Feiffer, Yearling-Random House, 1961.

44. graphic narratives: In many graphic narratives, both the illustrations and the text are created by one person; these kinds of works should be documented as in the first example below. Use the second example's format for works whose text is by one person and illustrations are by another.

Leavitt, Sarah. *Tangles: A Story about Alzheimer's, My Mother, and Me*. Freehand Books, 2010.

Butler, Octavia E. *Kindred: A Graphic Novel Adaptation.* Art by John Jennings, adapted by Damian Duffy, Abrams Books, 2017.

45. films or television episodes: These entries may be tailored to the context in which you are citing the work. If you are discussing the work of a director, for example, place the director's name in the Author element:

Medak, Peter, director. "The Buys." *The Wire*, created by David Simon and Ed Burns, season 1, episode 3, HBO, 16 June 2002.

Zhao, Chloé, director. *Nomadland.* Performances by Frances McDormand, Gay DeForest, Patricia Grier, and Linda May, Searchlight Pictures, 2020. *Hulu*, www.hulu.com/nomadland-movie.

If you are discussing a particular performance, place the actor's name in the Author element.

Moss, Elizabeth, performer. "A Little Kiss." *Mad Men*, directed by Jennifer Getzinger, AMC, 25 Mar. 2012.

Washington, Kerry, performer. "The Spark." *Little Fires Everywhere*, directed by Lynn Shelton, season 1, episode 1, Best Day Ever Productions et al., 2020. *Hulu*, www.hulu.com/series/little-fires-everywhere -bce24897-1a74-48a3-95e8-6cdd530dde4c.

46. online videos: If your source is a video on a website, cite, if you can, who uploaded the video, and the date on which the video was posted.

McDonald, Emily, director. *Looking Back with Pride.* Forever Pictures, 2021. *Vimeo*, uploaded by Emily McDonald, 21 June 2021, www.vimeo. com/565585933.

47. radio broadcasts:

> "Glenn Gould Special." *The Sunday Edition*, narrated by Robert Harris and Michael Enright, CBC Radio One, 23 Sept. 2012.

48. podcasts:

> "Are Young People Losing Faith in Democracy?" *Talking Politics*, hosted by David Runciman, 2 Nov. 2020, www.talkingpoliticspodcast.com/blog/2020/285-are -young-people-losing-faith-in-democracy.

49. recorded music:

> Bridgers, Phoebe. "Motion Sickness." *Stranger in the Alps*, Dead Oceans, 2017.

50. live performances: If you are citing a live performance or lecture, include the physical location and the city where the performance or lecture was delivered, as well as the date. Omit the city name if it is part of the location name. Include other information about the performance—the names of the director, the conductor, and/or lead performers, for instance—where such information is relevant. If your work focuses on the contribution of a performance's director, for example, cite that person in the Author element. Other important contributors follow the title in the Contributor element.

> Bedford, Brian, director. *The Importance of Being Earnest*. By Oscar Wilde, performances by Brian Bedford, Santino Fontana, David Furr, Charlotte Parry, and Sarah Topham, Roundabout Theater Company, 3 July 2011, American Airlines Theater, New York.

MLA Style

MacMillan, Margaret. "Hubris." *History's People: Person-alities and the Past*, 25 Sept. 2015, 7:00 p.m., Arts and Culture Centre, St. John's, NL. Massey Lecture.

51. works of visual art: When citing a physical object you have experienced, such as a work of art, provide in the Location element the name of the institution and city where you experienced it. Leave out the name of the city if the city name is part of the institution name (e.g., Art Institute of Chicago).

Belmore, Rebecca. *Fringe*. 2008, National Gallery of Canada, Ottawa.

Sargent, John Singer. *Henry James*. 1913, National Portrait Gallery, London.

If you access a work of art online or in a book, you should include full information about the website or volume you consulted.

Colquhoun, Ithell. *Scylla*. 1938, Tate Gallery, London. *Tate Women Artists*, by Alicia Foster, Tate, 2004, p. 85.

Giotto di Bondone. *Lamentation*. 1304–06, Capella Scrovegni, Padua. *Web Gallery of Art*, www.wga.hu/frames-e.html?/html/g/giotto/. Accessed 29 Jan. 2021.

52. interviews: Begin all entries for interviews with the name of the person being interviewed, and if there is a title for the interview, include it (in quotation marks if it is part of another work, or in italics if it has been published by itself). If there is no title, or if the title does not make clear that the work is an interview, write *Interview*, and give the name of the interviewer, if known. Finish with whatever publication information is appropriate. If you conducted the interview yourself, give the name of the person you interviewed, the medium (*Personal interview*, *Telephone interview*), and the date.

Lockwood, Patricia. "Patricia Lockwood Is a Good Reason to Never Log Off." Interview by Gabriella Paiella, *GQ*, 15 Feb. 2021, www.gq.com/story/patricia-lockwood-book-interview.

Rankine, Claudia. "The Art of Poetry No. 102." Interview by David L. Ulin, *Paris Review*, no. 219, winter 2016, www.theparisreview.org/interviews/6905/the-art-of-poetry-no-102-claudia-rankine.

Rosengarten, Herbert. Personal interview, 21 Jan. 2013.

53. online projects: In the case of large projects, cite the full range of years during which the project has been developed:

Secord, James A., et al., editors. *Darwin Correspondence Project*. 1974–2016, www.darwinproject.ac.uk/.

Willett, Perry, editor. *Victorian Women Writers Project*. Indiana University Digital Library Program, 1995–2016, webapp1/dlib.indiana.edu/vwwp/welcome.do. Accessed 26 Nov. 2021.

54. e-books: E-book citations should follow the basic pattern for physical books, with the format recorded in the Version element.

Edgeworth, Maria, et al. *Moral Tales: A Selection*. Edited by Robin Runia, e-book ed., Broadview Press, 2021.

Note that the above formatting applies to publications formatted for e-book web readers or e-readers. If you have accessed or downloaded an e-book from a website, digital platform, or database, format your citation as you would any other source found online, by adding a Container element and by citing a DOI or stable URL in the Location element.

> Austen, Jane. *Pride and Prejudice*. 1813. *Project Gutenberg*, 2008, www.gutenberg.org/files/1342/1342-h/1342 -h.htm. Accessed 20 Feb. 2021.

55. information databases:

> Morissette, René, et al. "Working from Home: Potential Implications for Public Transit and Greenhouse Gas Emissions." *Statistics Canada*, 22 Apr. 2021, https:// doi.org/10.25318/36280001202100400005-eng. Accessed 5 May 2021.

56. entry in a wiki: Wikis are online sites that can be added to and edited by any site user; as such, they may be subject to frequent changes made by any number of authors and editors. Do not, therefore, provide any authors' names. Start with the entry's title; then give the name of the wiki, the site publisher, the date of the entry's last update, the location, and the date you accessed the site.

> "William Caxton." *Wikipedia*. Wikimedia Foundation, 27 May 2021, www.en.wikipedia.org/wiki/ William_Caxton. Accessed 16 July 2021.

57. blog post: Include the title of the posting as your source title, the blog title as the first container, and the name of the blog host as a publisher.

> Gluck, Heather. "Brontë Society Fights to Keep 'Lost' Emily Brontë Poems Available for the Public."

> *MobyLives*, Melville House, 14 June 2021, www.
> mhpbooks.com/bronte-society-fights-to-keep
> -lost-emily-bronte-poems-available-for-the-public/.

58. e-mail message: Use the subject as the title and place it within quotation marks.

> Milton, Frank. "Thoughts on Animal Rights." Received
> by the author, 15 Jan. 2013.

If it is not clear from the context of your work that the source being cited is an e-mail, you may wish to add a supplemental element to the end of your citation that indicates the type of work.

> Stuart, Jennifer. "My Experience of the Attack." Received
> by the author, 17 May 2016. E-mail.

59. tweet: Copy the full, unchanged text of the tweet in the title element and enclose it in quotation marks. The username is included as the Author element.

> @TheAtlantic. "The president is loath to acknowledge
> that many Americans support the recent attacks on
> democracy, 'and those who don't face a system stacked
> against them,' @GrahamDavidA writes." *Twit-
> ter*, 14 July 2021, www.twitter.com/TheAtlantic/
> status/1415363709950701572.

60. comment posted on a web page: Usernames are given in full, unchanged. If the comment is anonymous, skip the author element. If the comment does not have its own title, provide instead a description of the comment that includes the title of the work being commented on (e.g., Comment on "Clinton Aims for Decisive Victory"). If it is available, include the exact time of posting in the Publication Date element.

Evan. Comment on "Another Impasse on Gun Bills, Another Win for Hyperpolitics." *The New York Times*, 21 June 2016, 9:02 a.m., www.nytimes. com/2016/06/22/us/politics/washington-congress -gun-control.html.

Among the details to notice in this referencing system:

- MLA style focuses on the process of documentation, not the prescriptive following of specific guidelines (though consistent formatting according to MLA principles is still vital to communicate clearly with your reader).

- To create a citation, list the relevant elements in the order prescribed by MLA (see the table on page 44). Any elements that don't apply to a given source are left out (placeholders for unknown information like *n.d.* ["no date"] are not required).

- Follow the punctuation guidelines in the table on page 44. Any elements recorded after a period should be capitalized; elements following a comma should be lower-case.

- Your citation should give your reader a map to your exact source. If you are documenting an article found in a periodical, for example, which was itself found on a database, you should include the publication details of both "containers" (periodical and database) as part of your citation. See the "Title of Container" section above for details.

- Terms such as *editor*, *edited by*, *translator*, *translated by*, and *review* are not abbreviated.

MLA Style

- If there are three or more authors or editors, only the first author's name is given, reversed, followed by *et al.*
- Citations for journals include abbreviations for volume and issue ("vol. 40, no. 3").
- Give the publisher's name in full, but drop business words such as "Company." For University presses, use the abbreviations *U*, *P*, and *UP*.
- City names are not required as part of the publication details.
- The date of access for an online source is optional.
- Page numbers are preceded by *p.* for a single page reference, or *pp.* for a range of pages.
- Include the URL (with *http:* removed) or the DOI in the location element for digital sources. Do not surround the address with angle brackets and do conclude with a period.
- You do not have to identify the media type of your source, unless it is required for clarity.

O *MLA Style Sample Essay*

Following is a sample essay written in MLA style. Note that further sample essays, some of which also employ MLA style, are available on the companion website associated with this book.

cover page
(not required
in MLA style,
but may be
required
by some
instructors)

Monumental Problems:

Setting the Criteria for Decisions in Political Aesthetics

By Robin Lee

Prof. K. D. Smith

Humanities 205

20 October 2021

all text
centered

name
and page
number
in top
right
corner

Robin Lee

Professor Smith

Humanities 205

20 October 2021

Monumental Problems:

Setting the Criteria for Decisions in Political Aesthetics

first line
of all
paragraphs
indented

text left-
justified
and
ragged
right

MLA Style

In recent years the level of political controversy over public monuments has greatly increased. Heated disagreements have arisen in America (over monuments honoring Confederate leaders and supporters of slavery); in Canada (over monuments honoring John A. Macdonald and other leaders of the past who were complicit in the ill-treatment of Indigenous Canadians); in Britain (over monuments honoring James Colston and other leaders of the past who were involved in the slave trade); and elsewhere around the world. Should these controversial monuments be removed? Should they be preserved but locked away, accessible only to historians and art historians? Should they be accessible to all, but be displayed in low-key fashion in museums or art galleries (with full contextualization provided) rather than be raised on pedestals in public places? Should they simply be destroyed as relics of a past we have moved beyond? Or should hard choices be made in individual cases, with some works preserved, some

Lee 2

not? In the heat of claims and counterclaims it can be difficult to sort out
what criteria are truly relevant for such decisions. This essay will examine
issues of relevance from several angles and will argue that one criterion in
particular deserves to be considered more frequently—the aesthetic value of
a work of art. Debates on these issues rightly include considerable discussion
of historical, political, and ethical issues, but too often entirely neglect
aesthetic considerations.

    It is important at the outset to recognize that cities, nations, and
cultures have been removing public monuments for almost as long as they
have been erecting them. In ancient Rome, for example, it was common to
remove and destroy monuments honoring one leader as soon as the next
one came to power; the Romans termed this process *damnatio memoriae*
or "condemnation of memory/legacy" (Byrne). The notion that societies
can and should periodically re-assess the leaders of the past and revise their
assessment of who deserves to be honored with public monuments is not an
idea dreamed up in the disrespectful twenty-first century; it has been with us
for millennia.

    Nor is it an idea that should be associated with any particular part of
the political spectrum. Some have suggested that it is predominantly those
on the political left who want to remove public monuments honoring
figures they feel do not deserve to be honored.[1] But the left has no
monopoly on such practices—far from it. Anti-communists joyously took
down thousands of statues of Soviet leaders after the fall of the Soviet

first paragraph ends with a statement of the essay's thesis

2

no page number given if unavailable

MLA Sty

3

endnote inserted to give additional information

Lee 3

Union in 1990. The Communist government of East Germany tore down statues of Wilhelm I (the first German Emperor) in 1950. Militaristic Canadians tore down a statue of the Kaiser in 1914, as Canada was going to war with Germany. Countries throughout Africa have removed public memorials to European colonial and imperialist figures. Back in 1912 the Kentucky chapter of the Daughters of the Confederacy was keen not only to erect a statue honoring Confederate leader Jefferson Davis but also to remove a statue of Abraham Lincoln in order to make way for Davis ("Objectionable"). And so it has gone; the idea of removing public monuments of discredited leaders is decidedly not something the radical left has dreamed up in our own era.

4   Nor is it a "freedom of speech" or "freedom of expression" issue, much as some have suggested that to be the case.[2] In Canada and the United States, as in democracies around the world, any individual remains free to commission and display in their front yard a statue of Robert E. Lee, of Joseph Stalin, or of whomever they like; the issue is whom governments decide (on behalf of the people as a whole) to honor with public monuments in civic squares, in public parks, or in front of legislatures and courthouses. Inevitably, views as to who deserves or does not deserve to be so honored change over time, and are often highly charged politically; consensus is often elusive.

5   One of the greatest mistakes of the debate over public monuments is to suppose that such monuments are intended primarily in order to

for a source listed by title, use a shortened title for parenthetical citation

text double-spaced throughout

MLA Style

Lee 4

preserve the historical record. On the contrary, statues placed on pedestals in prominent public places are placed there in order to honor those represented—and to invite the public to look up to them, both literally and figuratively.[3] The controversial Robert E. Lee monument in New Orleans, for example, "rose 109 feet. The bronze figure of Lee alone stood 16 feet tall and was hailed at the time as 'the largest bronze statue ever cast in New York'" (Cox 43).[4] Outsized statues of figures raised and presented in this fashion, then, are not *merely* statues of historical figures; they have become public monuments as well as statues. Such a statue is inevitably, as Benedito Machava of Yale University puts it, "a political statement" (Machava 00:03).

for audio and visual media works, use a time-stamp to locate the citation

Conversely, the act of removing a public monument in itself says nothing about history; there is no claim more absurd in the ongoing debate over public monuments than the frequently-made suggestion that removing a statue from a public place is tantamount to "erasing history."[5] The ways in which Jefferson Davis and Robert E. Lee shaped American history, and in which John A. Macdonald shaped Canadian history, are entirely unaffected by whether or not their statues are displayed in places of honor in our cities; their actions continue to be remembered, written about, and extensively discussed in schools and universities.

6

The reality is that arguments over the degree to which we may want to honor leaders of the past with public monuments today are first and foremost arguments about our political and ethical views and values today—not arguments about what happened decades or centuries ago. To be sure,

7

MLA Style

for indirect sources, use the abbreviation "qtd. in" ("quoted in")

those seeking to defend Macdonald downplay the policies that were designed to "do away with the tribal system and assimilate the Indian people in all respects" (qtd. in Beazley), just as those seeking to defend Lee and Davis downplay the extent to which these leaders were defenders of enslaving what Davis called "the servile race." But unrepentant racists aside (and it should be admitted that their numbers are not negligible), everyone acknowledges *both* that Macdonald played a central role in Canada's Confederation, *and* that his policies towards the Indigenous people in Canada were oppressive. The substantial disagreement is as to which values should be accorded more emphasis in our own time. Do we value the knitting together of a nation more than we deplore the oppression of its native peoples? Similarly, it is broadly agreed *both* that Robert E. Lee and Jefferson Davis were defenders of slavery who were themselves enslavers *and* that they were well-mannered and behaved graciously in defeat. The substantial disagreement is again as to what values should be accorded more emphasis in our own time. Do we value graciousness in defeat more than we deplore the slavery and subsequent oppression of a substantial portion of a nation's people?

8   Other values too are at stake in these controversies. In fighting for slavery (and "states' rights"),[6] for example, Davis and Lee were also fighting against federal interference in an economic system according to the principles of which those with vast amounts of capital should be allowed to do what they wish with it.[7] That fight too has a powerful echo in debates in America today (and, indeed, around the world); to what degree should

MLA Style

a belief in the desirability of all humans being treated equitably outweigh a belief that capitalism should be allowed free rein?

Not everything, of course, can or should be seen only through the lens of today. Those who say we should not assess historical figures entirely by the standards of today make a fair point; we need to understand the ways in which earlier eras differed from our own. It would be obviously absurd to argue that John A. Macdonald or Woodrow Wilson should be disparaged because they did not support gay rights, when no one in late nineteenth- or early twentieth-century North America contemplated equal rights on the basis of sexual orientation. We need to understand too that "the standards of the past" are never uniform. During the same decade that Woodrow Wilson was doing everything in his power while President of Princeton to keep African Americans from attending that university, the presidents of Columbia and Yale were for the first time welcoming African Americans into those institutions. On the matter of Macdonald's Conservative government setting up the oppressive system of Indigenous residential schools, it seems fair to point out that very few in mainstream white society at the time opposed his action; when Wilfrid Laurier's Liberals came to power, indeed, they greatly expanded the system (and it was under Laurier's successor, Robert Borden, that it was made compulsory under the Indian Act for all Indigenous children to attend either industrial or residential schools). It seems fair to point out too that the attitudes adopted by Macdonald and other Canadian politicians of the 1870s were in many

9

MLA Style

respects considerably less oppressive than those adopted by their American counterparts at the time; no one in Macdonald's government was making statements as extreme as American Congressman James Michael Cavanaugh's 1868 assertion: "I have never in my life seen a good Indian except when I have seen a dead Indian" (Mieder 42). When it comes to the matter of public monuments, discussion will inevitably focus less on achieving entirely balanced assessments of how individuals behaved in the context of their own time than on questions of who (and of what sorts of behavior) we wish to *honor* in the present. But our answers to those questions may sometimes be appropriately shaded in one direction or the other to the extent that they are informed by an awareness of history's nuances.

parenthetical references at end of short quotations followed by punctuation

10   Even more important is that our judgments on such matters should be informed by an awareness of social psychology. When Indigenous Canadians such as Marie Knockwood (a member of the Abegweit First Nation who was taken from her home in Prince Edward Island and forced to attend the Shubenacadie Residential School in Nova Scotia when she was 10 years old) testify that they feel "full of anger and bitterness" (MacLeod) when they see Macdonald honored with public monuments, it matters. When African Americans such as Nicole Moliere of New Orleans testify that walking or driving past statues of the likes of Lee and Davis feels like "a daily assault" (qtd. in O'Neal), it matters.

11   Such concerns were very much on the minds of the New Orleans City Council and Mayor Mitch Landrieu when they decided in 2017 to remove

the Lee and Davis monuments—along with a number of other Confederate
monuments.[8] At the moment they remain in storage, awaiting a final
decision as to where or if they should again be displayed.

How should the fate of such statues be decided? And what
considerations should be given most weight in reaching those decisions?
Sathnam Sanghera is among those who have suggested that, in the case
of many British colonial monuments, at least, it may be better to leave
monuments where they are and to "level the playing field" not by destroying
old monuments but by erecting new monuments alongside them to present
the other side of the story (167). As a purely practical matter, however, it
would surely take many decades to "level the playing field" in this way.
Moreover, the approach Sanghera recommends would continue to invite the
public to revere many figures who, most people now agree, do not deserve to
be so honored.

Many have suggested that all such monuments should still be displayed
publicly, but in a venue such as a museum where they can be accompanied
by full contextualization, and where their placement does not suggest that
they are to be regarded with veneration. That indeed seems an attractive
solution—until one considers all the implications. Consider for one thing
the financial implications. Art historian Erin L. Thompson is one scholar
who has done exactly that—and she argues persuasively against preservation.
She references an investigation that concluded "that in the previous ten
years, taxpayers had spent at least 40 million dollars preserving Confederate

12

13

MLA Style

Lee 9

monuments," and she draws attention as well to the added cost of displaying
them in museums rather than in public as monuments:

> [At the University of North Carolina], when protesters in 2018
> tore down the "Silent Sam" Confederate statue (see fig. 7),
> U.N.C. proposed building a new museum to house it that would
> cost over five million dollars and almost a million dollars a year
> in ongoing maintenance and security. So I look at these statues
> as money sinks. And I think about all of the amazing sites of
> African-American history or Native American history that are
> disintegrating from lack of funding and think those dollars could
> be better spent elsewhere. (Qtd. in Bromwich)

in-text
citation fol-
lowing block
quotation
comes after
final punctua-
tion and no
punctuation
follows

Thompson makes an important point; re-deploying all the problematic
monuments within museums would be extraordinarily expensive. But it
would surely be an extreme measure not to preserve *any* of them. How, then,
should societies choose?

MLA Style

14   At this point it seems to me important to consider one more
truth about these public monuments. We have noted the importance of
acknowledging that such monuments make political statements. We have
noted too the need for decisions regarding such monuments to be informed
not only by today's values and today's politics but also by an awareness of
history and an awareness of social psychology. We need further to remember
that when statues acquire the status of public monuments, they do not cease
to be statues. They do not cease, that is to say, to be *aesthetic* objects. This

aesthetic side is more often than not entirely forgotten, as politically charged discussions about them become more and more heated.[9] But it is vitally important to keep it in mind when societies take statues off their pedestals and try to decide the fate of what were *formerly* public monuments.

To open discussion of the aesthetic element, I would like to consider a case over which debate has been rather less heated than have been many of the arguments over statues of Confederate leaders—or, indeed, over statues of Macdonald. The largest monument issue in the continent's largest city has involved a president often praised for his aggressive "trust busting" and for other progressive policies—Theodore Roosevelt. On racial issues, Roosevelt's record is mixed; undeniably racist in some respects, he was arguably rather less so than most white Americans of his era—and certainly quite considerably less so than was his successor, Woodrow Wilson. But a mixed record on such issues by the standards of a hundred years ago is not likely to lead to a twenty-first-century consensus that one deserves to be put on a pedestal.

Roosevelt was an important benefactor of the Museum of Natural History, and when he died the Memorial Association created by the New York State Legislature recommended that the museum would be the most appropriate location for a memorial honoring him.[10] Eventually the nature of the monument itself was decided on, and the various parties—the Memorial Association, the New York State legislature, and the American Museum of Natural History Board of Trustees (which included

15

16

MLA Style

Lee 11

representatives of the Roosevelt family)—together specified that the monument should be made up of "an equestrian statue of Roosevelt with two accompanying figures on foot, one an American Indian and the other a native African, representing his gun bearers and suggestive of Roosevelt's interest in the original peoples of these widely separated countries" (qtd. in Marber 93). In a sentence quoted much less frequently, they specified as well the imposing height of the monument: "this group [of figures] will rise to a height of 30 feet above the sidewalk" (Freundlich 123). They commissioned James Earle Fraser—at the time acclaimed as one of the nation's finest sculptors—to create the work. When the statue (see fig. 1 and fig. 2) was finally unveiled, Fraser provided his own description of the group of figures and their significance: "The two figures at [Roosevelt's] side are guides symbolizing the continents of Africa and America, and if you choose may stand for Roosevelt's friendliness to all races" (American Museum of Natural History, "What Did").

MLA Style

when citing two or more works by the same author, add a title to the in-text citation, shortened if necessary

Fig. 1. James Earle Fraser, *Equestrian Statue of Theodore Roosevelt* (front view detail), 1939.

MLA Style

partial
bib-
liographic
details for
figures
and tables
can be
included
in the
caption,
with full
details
in the
Works
Cited list
(as here)

Fig. 2. James Earle Fraser, *Equestrian Statue of Theodore Roosevelt* (side view detail), 1939.

MLA Style

17   That is not, of course, how many perceive the relationship among the three figures today. The positioning of the figures, as the statement issued by the museum when they decided in 2020 to remove the statue put it, "communicates a racial hierarchy that the museum and members of the public have long found disturbing" (American Museum of Natural History, "Addressing the Statue"). That judgment is surely correct; regardless of Fraser's original intent or the intent of those who commissioned him to create the work, there can be no doubt the arrangement of the figures

suggests to many minds—certainly including many African American and Indigenous American minds—a relationship in which the white man is regarded as inherently superior, the other two inherently inferior. In removing the statue from its prominent place on a triple pedestal outside the front of the museum, they did nothing to "erase history." What they did was to change the status of the object. Removed from its place of honor as a public monument, it loses that status; it becomes simply a statue. For the moment that statue—like the New Orleans statues of Lee and Davis—is in storage, awaiting a final decision as to its long-term fate. Is it a statue that deserves to be preserved? Let us set ethics and politics to one side for a moment, and pay some attention to aesthetics.

To begin with, we should acknowledge that the fashion in which the three humans and the horse are arranged—much as it portrays a hierarchy that we now rightly understand to be inappropriate—is quite striking visually. All three figures are rendered in entirely lifelike fashion; the positioning of the limbs, the musculature, the facial expressions—in every respect these figures feel human. But more than that, they feel—to me at least—like interesting humans. Clearly heroism is intended to be celebrated here in the presentation of all three figures, but that is surely not all that is conveyed. Along with the heroic determination of the conqueror, is there not in Roosevelt's expression something of arrogance, and of ruthlessness? The expressions of the two other figures are more difficult to read. Strength and determination, certainly. Stoicism? Perhaps. And pride—especially in

18

Lee 15

the face of the Native American figure. Can hints of sorrow be detected behind the surface of these faces? And is there a hint, especially in the face of the African, of a strength and determination that could readily be refocused into resistance against the conqueror? In short, all three faces have to them a good deal of complexity—an extraordinary amount of complexity, given that the heroic genre necessitates a substantial degree of idealization in the presentation. All three offer the viewer a good deal to reflect on, and are capable of sparking thoughts that go against the grain of a statue that may seem at first to be a straightforward idealization of an historical figure. The entire work, indeed, is capable of sparking such thoughts. Look, for example, at the way in which Roosevelt is pulling hard on the horse's double reins—here too we can sense a hint more of cruelty than of heroism. In the words of Art History professor Harriet F. Senie of The City College of New York, "the Fraser sculpture is a good work of art by any artistic standards" (American Museum of Natural History, "Perspectives").[11] It surely deserves to be preserved—and, in some appropriate venue, at some point in the future, made available to the public again.

19   As it happens, Fraser's spouse, Laura Gardin Fraser, was also among the leading sculptors of the era—and her work too has been embroiled in controversy. Here again it is worth considering the aesthetic side of the argument. Perhaps her best-known work is her 1946 statue (figs. 3–6) depicting Robert E. Lee and Stonewall Jackson on their way to the battle of Chancellorsville. The first double equestrian statue to be completed

Lee 16

in America, it stood for many decades as a monument in Wyman Park in Baltimore, mounted on a large pedestal. At its base were various inscriptions celebrating Lee and Jackson as "Christian soldiers" who "waged war like gentlemen" ("Lee Jackson Monument"). In 2017, following the recommendation of a special commission appointed by the city, the statue was removed and placed in storage.

Fig. 3. Laura Gardin Fraser, *Stonewall Jackson and Robert E. Lee Monument* (front view detail), 1948.

Fig. 4. Laura Gardin Fraser, *Stonewall Jackson and Robert E. Lee Monument* (close up detail of Jackson), 1948.

Fig. 5. Laura Gardin Fraser, *Stonewall Jackson and Robert E. Lee Monument* (close up detail of Lee), 1948.

Fig. 6. *Laura Gardin Fraser in Her Studio at Work on Model for "Lee-Jackson Monument,"* c. 1947.

Again, let us set ethics and politics aside for a moment and consider   20
aesthetics. It is difficult not to be struck immediately by the lifelike
quality of Fraser's sculpting. The figures feel as if they are in motion, and
every detail—the feet in the stirrups, the hands on the binoculars—feels
convincing. Many equestrian statues have a static quality to them; this one
feels entirely dynamic. And the expressions of the figures have considerable
depth and complexity to them—Lee has a calm, almost impassive façade
on his features, while Jackson's expression conveys a rougher sort of
determination that perhaps hints as well at the ferocity of his religious

devotion and his devotion to military discipline. The sculpting has the power to suggest a wide range of thoughts as to how these men would be inclined to act as generals—and, indeed, as husbands, fathers, and enslavers. Perhaps even more striking, though, is the overall composition of the work. The way in which the figures—equine as well as human—are placed together is highly artistic, even as it feels entirely natural; the lines and the curves of the figures convey an extraordinary sense of peacefulness and harmony. That the relationship between the two generals was extremely close is well-known— Lee is said to have remarked that he lost his right arm when Jackson died. And yet there is a powerful tension underlying this harmony; however strong the relationship between them, these are generals who are about to lead their troops into a battle in which thousands will die.

21   Fraser spent twelve years working on the statue; it shows. On aesthetic grounds alone, I would argue that this is a work worth preserving, worth contextualizing, and worth making available to the public.

22   Spending some time on the aesthetics of statues such as these sets the aesthetic qualities of a number of other statues that have been the subject of controversy into bold relief. Illustrated below are the "Silent Sam" UNC monument (fig. 7) of an anonymous Confederate soldier that Erin L. Thompson references; the New Orleans monument in honor of Jefferson Davis (fig. 8) that was removed in 2017; and a Regina, Saskatchewan monument in honor of John A. Macdonald (fig. 9) that was removed in April 2021. The figure in the UNC monument is not an obviously poor

Lee 20

work, but nor is it strikingly accomplished; the face is blandly inexpressive and the figure has a static, posed feeling to it. The New Orleans Davis statue seems to me to have little to recommend it aesthetically either. Arching backwards but with one arm thrown forward, Davis is presumably meant to look heroic, but his pose seems awkward and ungainly. Awkward arm extension is an aesthetic issue too with the Regina monument to Macdonald. That monument, which dates from 1967, was controversial at that time for aesthetic rather than political reasons; one local gallery curator called it "commonplace," a "caricature" that "tells us absolutely nothing about the character of the man," while another (Ronald Bloore, who would soon become a nationally-known artist) described it as a work that "totally lacks artistic merit" (qtd. in Martin). What's more—as a comparison with photographs of Macdonald makes very clear—the work bears very little resemblance to the person being portrayed.

sentence structured so that it flows grammatically into quotation

MLA Style

Lee 21

Fig. 7. John A. Wilson, *Silent Sam*, 1913.

Fig. 8. Edward Virginius Valentine, *Jefferson Davis Monument*, 1911.

Lee 22

Fig. 9. Sonia de Grandmaison, *John A. Macdonald Memorial* (detail), 1967.

Whereas the aesthetic case is extremely strong for the preservation

23

in perpetuity of works such as James Earle Fraser's equestrian statue of

Roosevelt and Laura Gardin Fraser's double equestrian statue of Lee and

Jackson, the aesthetic case for the preservation in perpetuity of these

other works is surely much weaker. The case is particularly weak for its

preservation in perpetuity *at public expense*. Resources for such things

are always in short supply, and (as Thompson suggests) there is a strong

argument for giving priority when distributing those scarce resources to

those who have been disadvantaged in the past—to providing funds to

Lee 23

support Indigenous and Black sculptors today, and to providing funds to support the creation of work honoring heroic figures from the past who were never in earlier eras considered fit subjects for public monuments. Before we commit—at very considerable expense—to preserving all of the many hundreds of monuments erected in honor of Lee and Davis, and all of the dozens of monuments erected in honor of Macdonald, we should surely commit to balancing the scales. Before we commit to funding the placing of a contextualized Lee and a contextualized Davis in every American museum and of a contextualized Macdonald in every Canadian one, we should surely look to commission more monuments honoring Frederick Douglass and Harriet Tubman, Mary Shadd and Ida Wells, Tecumseh and Sitting Bull.[12]

24   In the current climate it may well be needlessly divisive to destroy any statues—even those statues that have little or no interest or historical importance, and little claim to aesthetic merit. To store them away at the lowest possible expense for another generation or two may well be the most advisable solution for the present. But let us not commit to the preservation of all these monuments in perpetuity; when it comes time to display some of these pieces in contextualized fashion in museum settings, let us be selective in choosing for preservation only the most interesting, the most important, and the most valuable aesthetically.

MLA Style

final paragraph restates and broadens the essay's main argument

Notes

1   Limbaugh, for example, links the movement to remove
monuments to "the American and the worldwide left."

2   Donald Trump is a notable example. As Macaya et al. report,
he made the following statement about the removal of Confederate
monuments during a speech he delivered in Tulsa: "This cruel campaign
of censorship and exclusion violates everything we hold dear as
Americans." When Virginia's governor announced the state's intention
to take down a prominent public memorial to Robert E. Lee, state
senator Amanda Chase argued that, because such monuments are a form
of artistic expression, removing them raises "First Amendment concerns"
(Carrington and Strother). In Canada, former journalist Robert Roth
is among those who contend that taking down public monuments
honoring former prime ministers is "to suppress free speech" (Llana).

3   An exception is John Dann's statue of Sir John A. Macdonald,
which was removed from its place in front of Victoria's City Hall in
2017. Dann has drawn attention to the fact that in this case the statue
was not raised high above the street level but rather placed at eye level
with passers-by: "It's not a sculpture on a pedestal, it's not a monument.
It's a portrait of a man and that man is accessible to the people who go
in and out of the building" (Canadian Press).

4   Also relevant is the location of such monuments. As Rebecca
Shehan and Jennifer Speights-Binet point out, "The monuments

*notes
numbered
as in text*

*each note
indented*

MLA Style

held prominent locations in highly traveled areas—their adjacency
to quotidian traffic underpinned the taken-for-grantedness of white
supremacy" (351).

5   See, for example, Constantine, "Ignoring American History,"
and Caplan, "Huckabee."

6   It seems appropriate to put the term "states' rights" in
quotation marks here; the vast majority of reputable historians now see
the argument that was long put forward by Southern whites—that the
central issue in the Civil War was "states' rights" (rather than slavery)—
is at best a smokescreen, and at worst an outright lie.

7   Jefferson Davis made the matter clear in his 29 April 1861
speech to the Confederate Congress: "The South were willing purchasers
of property suitable to their wants, and paid the price of the acquisition
without harboring a suspicion that their quiet possession was to be
disturbed" (Ainsworth and Kirkley 258).

8   Landrieu's speech explaining how he had become convinced
that removing the monuments was the right thing to do received
national coverage. The explanation touched extensively on the personal:
"Another friend asked me to consider these four monuments from the
perspective of an African American mother or father trying to explain
to their fifth-grade daughter who Robert E. Lee is and why he stands
atop of our beautiful city. Can you do it? Can you look into that young
girl's eyes and convince her that Robert E. Lee is there to encourage

MLA Style

her? Do you think she will feel inspired and hopeful by that story? Do these monuments help her see a future with limitless potential? Have you ever thought that if her potential is limited, yours and mine are too? We all know the answer to these very simple questions. When you look into this child's eyes is the moment when the searing truth comes into focus for us. This is the moment when we know what is right and what we must do. We can't walk away from this truth. We must always remember our history and learn from it. But that doesn't mean we must valorize the ugliest chapters, as we do when we put the Confederacy on a pedestal—literally—in our most prominent public places" (Landrieu).

9   If the aesthetic aspect is touched on at all, it tends to be in an aside in which the aesthetic value (or lack thereof) of a work is merely asserted, rather than discussed in any extended fashion. Such is the case, for example, with the offhand reference in an *Economist* column concerning a statue of Cecil Rhodes outside of Oxford University's Oriel College, in which the columnist asserts the statue to be "ugly" (Bagehot).

10   The original plan was not, however, to locate the memorial on the steps of the museum; it was rather to include it adjacent to the museum, as part of a promenade through Central Park that would have linked the American Museum of Natural History with the Metropolitan Museum of Art (Reynolds).

11   Marber is one other scholar who has expressed a view on the aesthetics of the issue: "Additionally, it is undeniable that the Equestrian Statue has inherent artistic and art-historical merit" (95).

12   It is striking that Gabriel Koren, one of the very few sculptors to have made statues of prominent African Americans a specialty (her statue of Frederick Douglass stands in New York's Central Park), has experienced considerable financial difficulty; in 2015 she was forced out of her Brooklyn studio, no longer able to afford the rent (Swarns).

Works Cited

Ainsworth, Fred C., and Joseph W. Kirkley, eds. *The War of the Rebellion: A Compilation of the Official Records of the Union and Confederate Armies.* Series 4, vol. 1, Government Printing Office, 1900, www.books.google.ca/books. Accessed 14 July 2021.

American Museum of Natural History. "Addressing the Statue." Statement. *American Museum of Natural History*, June 2020, www.amnh.org/exhibitions/addressing-the-theodore-roosevelt-statue#statement. Accessed 19 May 2021.

——. "Perspectives on the Statue." *American Museum of Natural History*, www.amnh.org/exhibitions/addressing-the-theodore-roosevelt-statue/perspectives-today. Accessed 18 July 2021.

——. "What Did the Artists and Planners Intend?" *American Museum of Natural History*, www.amnh.org/exhibitions/addressing-the-theodore-roosevelt-statue/making-the-statue. Accessed 18 July 2021.

Bagehot [Adrian Woolridge]. "Britain's Academic Split: Problem-solving v Problem-wallowing." *The Economist,* 19 June 2021, www.economist.com/britain/2021/06/19/britains-academic-split-problem-solving-v-problem-wallowing. Accessed 14 July 2021.

Beazley, Doug. "Decolonizing the Indian Act." *National Magazine*, Canadian Bar Association, 18 Dec. 2017, www.nationalmagazine.ca/en-ca/articles/law/in-depth/2017/decolonizing-the-indian-act.

each entry begins at left margin; subsequent lines are indented

MLA recommends truncating excessively long URLs after host location

MLA Style

works cited are listed alphabetically

MLA Style

Accessed 13 July 2021.

double spacing used throughout

Bromwich, Jonah Engel. "What Does It Take to Tear Down a Statue?" Interview with Erin L. Thompson. *New York Times*, 11 June 2020, www.nytimes.com/2020/06/11/style/confederate-statue-columbus-analysis.html. Accessed 12 July 2021.

Byrne, Patrick. "Americans Channel Ancient Rome in Condemning Confederate Statues." *The Hill*, 23 Aug. 2017, www.thehill.com/blogs/pundits-blog/state-local-politics/347562-americans-channel-ancient-rome-in-erecting-statues. Accessed 10 Mar. 2021.

Canadian Press. "Vancouver Artist of Removed Macdonald Statue Says It Was Never Intended as a Monument." 15 Aug. 2018, www.lethbridgenewsnow.com/2018/08/15/artist-behind-macdonald-statue-says-it-was-never-intended-as-a-monument/. Accessed 13 July 2021.

Caplan, Talia. "Huckabee: Erasing American History Is 'Dangerous,' Can Lead to a Lost Civilization." *Fox News*, 23 June 2021, www.foxnews.com/media/huckabee-erasing-history-dangerous-can-lead-lost-civilization. Accessed 14 July 2021.

italics used for titles of books, journals, magazines, etc.

Carrington, Nathan T., and Logan Strother, "Legally, Confederate Statues in Public Spaces Aren't a Form of Free Speech." *Newsday*, 20 June 2020, www.newsday.com/opinion/commentary/confederate-statues-free-speech-black-lives-matter-protests-racism-1.45750735. Accessed 10 July 2021.

Constantine, Tim. "Ignoring American History Is Dangerous." *Washington Times*, 12 June 2021, www.washingtontimes.com/news/2020/jun/12/ignoring-american-history-is-dangerous/. Accessed 12 July 2021.

Cox, Karen L. *No Common Ground: Confederate Monuments and the Ongoing Fight for Racial Justice.* U of North Carolina P, 2021.

Fraser, James Earle. *Equestrian Statue of Theodore Roosevelt* (front view detail). 1939, New York City. Photograph by Roberto Machado Noa, 2020, www.medium.com/the-polis/statues-arent-about-preserving-history.

——. *Equestrian Statue of Theodore Roosevelt* (side view detail). 1939, New York City. Photograph by LunchboxLarry, 2013, www.commons.wikimedia.org/wiki/File:Equestrian_statue_of_Theodore_Roosevelt.jpg.

Fraser, Laura Gardin. *Stonewall Jackson and Robert E. Lee Monument.* 1948, Baltimore. Photograph by Jerry Jackson, *Baltimore Sun*, 2015, www.baltimoresun.com/opinion/op-ed/bs-ed-confederate-lessons-20151027-story.html.

——. *Stonewall Jackson and Robert E. Lee Monument* (close up detail of Jackson), 1948, Baltimore. Photograph by C. Ryan Patterson, in *Special Commission to Review Baltimore's Public Confederate Monuments*, 2016, www.baltimoreplanning.wixsite.com/monumentcommission/.

—. *Stonewall Jackson and Robert E. Lee Monument* (close up detail of Lee), 1948, Baltimore. Photograph by C. Ryan Patterson, in *Special Commission to Review Baltimore's Public Confederate Monuments*, 2016, www.baltimoreplanning.wixsite.com/ monumentcommission/.

Freundlich, A.L. *The Sculpture of James Earle Fraser.* Universal Publishers, 2001.

Grandmaison, Sonia de. *John A. Macdonald Memorial.* 1967, Regina, Saskatchewan. Photograph by Scotwood 72, Wikimedia Commons, 2006, www.commons.wikimedia.org/wiki/ File:Macdonaldstat.jpg.

Landrieu, Mitch. "Speech on the Removal of Confederate Monuments in New Orleans." Transcript. *New York Times*, 23 May 2017, www. nytimes.com/2017/05/23/opinion/mitch-landrieus-speech -transcript.html. Accessed 18 July 2021.

"Laura Gardin Fraser in Her Studio at Work on Model for 'Lee-Jackson Monument.'" c. 1947, www.nationalcowboymuseum. org/explore/art-sculpture/.

"Lee Jackson Monument, 1948." *Special Commission to Review Baltimore's Public Confederate Monuments.* www.baltimoreplanning. wixsite.com/monumentcommission/leeandjacksonmonument. Accessed 18 July 2021.

Limbaugh, Rush. "Limbaugh to Activists Targeting Historical Monuments."

Washington Times, 15 Aug. 2017, www.washingtontimes.
com/news/2017/aug/15/rush-limbaugh-to-activists-targeting
-historical-mo/. Accessed 8 Feb. 2021.

Llana, Sara Miller. "Canada's Founder Oppressed Indigenous Peoples.
Should His Statues Stand?" *Christian Science Monitor*, 19 Oct. 2020,
www.csmonitor.com/World/Americas/2020/1019/. Accessed 14 July
2021.

Macaya, Melissa, et al. "Trump Holds Rally in Tulsa, Oklahoma." *CNN*, 21
June 2020, www.cnn.com/politics/live-news/trump
-rally-tulsa-oklahoma/. Accessed 20 May 2021.

Machava, Benedito. "The Fate of Africa's Colonial Statues." *YouTube*, n.d.,
https://www.youtube.com/watch?v=GO6qduD3hd4. Accessed 14 July
2021.

MacLeod, Nicola. "Residential School Survivor Says P.E.I. John A.
Macdonald Statue Should Be Removed." *CBC News*, 11 Sept. 2020,
www.cbc.ca/news/canada/prince-edward-island/pei-marie
-knockwood-john-a-macdonald-statue-1.5719669. Accessed 30 June
2021. Video.

Marber, Sinclaire Devereux. "Bloody Foundation? Ethical and Legal
Foundations of (Not) Removing the Equestrian Statue of Theodore
Roosevelt at the American Museum of Natural History." *Columbia
Journal of Law and the Arts*, vol. 43, no. 1, Dec. 2019, www.journals.
library.columbia.edu/index.php/lawandarts/article/

view/4126. Accessed 23 May 2021.

Martin, Ashley. "Regina's John A. Macdonald Statue: Looking Back, Looking Forward." *Regina Leader Post*, 18 Sept. 2020, www.leaderpost.com/news/local-news/reginas-john-a-macdonald-statue-looking-back-looking-forward. Accessed 15 July 2021.

Mieder, Wolfgang. "'The Only Good Indian Is a Dead Indian': History and Meaning of a Proverbial Stereotype." *The Journal of American Folklore*, vol. 106, no. 419, winter 1993, pp. 38-60. *JSTOR*, www.jstor.org/stable/541345?read-now=1&seq=4#page_scan_tab_contents.

"Objectionable to Kentucky Confederate Daughters." *Kentucky Messenger-Inquirer*, 15 Nov. 1912, www.newspapers.com/image/375908902/.

O'Neal, Lonnae. "New Orleans, Robert E. Lee, and the South's Treasonous History of Alternative Facts." *The Undefeated*, 22 May 2017, www.theundefeated.com/features/new-orleans-robert-e-lee-highway/. Accessed 18 June 2021.

Reynolds, Donald Martin. "The Original Plan for the Theodore Roosevelt Monument." *Sculpture Review*, 8 Oct. 2020, https://doi.org/10.1177/0747528420967271.

Sanghera, Sathnam. *Empireland: How Imperialism Has Shaped Modern Britain*. Viking, 2021.

Shehan, Rebecca, and Jennifer Speights-Binet. "Negotiating Strategies in New Orleans's Memory-work: White Fragility in the Politics of

Removing Four Confederate-inspired Monuments." *Journal of Cultural Geography*, vol. 36, no. 3, 2019, pp. 346-67. https://doi:10.1080/08873631.2019.1641996.

Swarns, Rachel L. "Priced Out of Brooklyn, a Sculptor Seeks a New Studio to Rent." *New York Times*, 16 Aug. 2015, www.nytimes.com/2015/08/17/nyregion/priced-out-of-brooklyn-a-sculptor-seeks-a-new-studio-to-rent.html. Accessed 18 July 2021.

Valentine, Edward Virginius. *Jefferson Davis Monument*. 1911, New Orleans. Photograph by Ashley Merlin for the New Orleans Monumental Task Committee, 2015.

Wilson, John A. *Silent Sam*. 1913, Chapel Hill, North Carolina. Photograph, 2012, www.commons.wikimedia.org/wiki/File:SilentSambyJohnAWilson.tif.

APA Style

Incorporating Sources in APA Style   123
Summarizing   124
Paraphrasing   125
Quoting Directly   127
  Formatting Quotations   128
    Adding to or Deleting from a Quotation   130
    Integrating Quotations   132
Signal Phrases   133

About In-Text Citations   135
1.   in-text citation   135
2.   no signal phrase (or author not named in signal phrase)   137
3.   titles of stand-alone works   137
4.   titles of articles and chapters of books   138
5.   placing of in-text citations   138
6.   citations when text is in parentheses   139
7.   electronic source—page number unavailable   139
8.   audiovisual works   140
9.   two or more dates for a work   140
10. two authors   141
11. three or more authors   141
12. organization as author   142
13. author not given   142
14. date not given   142
15. two or more works in the same citation   142
16. two or more authors with the same last name   143
17. works in a collection of readings or anthology   143
18. indirect source   144
19. personal communications   145
20. Indigenous traditional knowledge and oral traditions   145

About References   146
21. work with single author   148
22. two authors   148
23. three to twenty authors   148
24. more than twenty authors   149
25. works with an organization as author   149
26. works with unknown author   149
27. two or more works by the same author   150
28. two or more works by the same author in the same year   150
29. prefaces, introductions, forewords, afterwords   151

APA Style

30.	edited works	151
31.	works with an author and a translator	151
32.	selections from edited books and collections of readings	151
33.	selections from multivolume works	152
34.	ebooks and audiobooks	152
35.	periodical articles (with and without DOIs)	152
36.	abstract of a periodical article	154
37.	magazine articles	154
38.	newspaper articles	154
39.	reviews	155
40.	reference work entries with an individual author	155
41.	reference work entries with an organization as author	155
42.	diagnostic manuals (DSM and ICD)	156
43.	articles from databases	156
44.	dissertations from a database, published and unpublished	157
45.	data sets	158
46.	software and reference apps	158
47.	films and video recordings	158
48.	episodes from television series	159
49.	TED Talks	159
50.	YouTube and other streaming videos	159
51.	podcasts	160
52.	music recordings	160
53.	recorded webinars	161
54.	interviews	161
55.	blog posts	161
56.	Wikipedia article	162
57.	social media	162
58.	Facebook posts	163
59.	Instagram photos or videos	163
60.	tweets	163
61.	other webpages and websites	164
62.	visual works	164
63.	work of art in a gallery or gallery website	164
64.	stock images or clip art	165
65.	infographics	165
66.	maps	165
67.	photographs	165
68.	PowerPoint slides, lecture notes, recorded Zoom lectures	166
69.	conference presentations	166
	APA Style Sample Essay	168

APA Style

◎ APA Style

The American Psychological Association (APA) style is used in many scientific, health, behavioral science, and social science disciplines. APA style calls for parenthetical references in the body of a paper; the main components in these are author, date, and (possibly) page or paragraph number. APA also requires that full bibliographical information about the sources be provided in a list called "References" at the end of the essay.

This section outlines the key features of APA style and includes, at the end, a full sample essay using APA citation. Additional full sample essays in APA style are available on the Broadview website. Go to http://sites.broadviewpress.com/writing/. If you have more detailed questions, consult *The Publication Manual of the American Psychological Association* (7th edition, 2020). You may also find answers at www.apastyle.org.

O *Incorporating Sources in APA Style*

The following material should be read in conjunction with the introductory discussion of citation, documentation, and plagiarism (see pages 11–30).

There are three main ways of working source material into a paper: summaries, paraphrases, and direct quotations. In order to avoid plagiarism, care must be taken with all three kinds of borrowing, both in the way they are handled and in their referencing. In what follows, a passage from page 102 of a book by Terrence W. Deacon (*The Symbolic Species: The Co-Evolution of Language and the Brain*,

APA Style

published by Norton in 1997) serves as the source for a sample summary, paraphrase, and quotation. The examples feature the APA style of in-text parenthetical citations, but the requirements for presenting the source material are the same for all academic referencing systems.

original source   Over the last few decades language researchers seem to have reached a consensus that language is an innate ability, and that only a significant contribution from innate knowledge can explain our ability to learn such a complex communication system. Without question, children enter the world predisposed to learn human languages. All normal children, raised in normal social environments, inevitably learn their local language, whereas other species, even when raised and taught in this same environment, do not. This demonstrates that human brains come into the world specially equipped for this function.

O *Summarizing*

An honest and competent summary, whether of a passage or an entire book, must not only represent the source accurately but also use original wording and include a citation. It is a common misconception that only quotations need to be acknowledged as borrowings in the body of an essay, but without a citation, even a fairly worded summary or paraphrase is an act of plagiarism. The first example below is faulty on two counts: it borrows wording (underlined) from the source, and it has no parenthetical reference.

needs checking   <u>Researchers</u> agree that language learning is <u>innate, and that only innate knowledge can</u>

explain how we are able <u>to learn</u> a <u>system</u> of <u>communication</u> that is so <u>complex</u>. <u>Normal children raised in normal</u> ways will always <u>learn their local language</u>, <u>whereas other species do not, even when taught</u> human language and exposed to the <u>same environment</u>.

The next example avoids the wording of the source passage, and a parenthetical citation notes the author and date. APA does not require that page or paragraph numbers be provided in summarized material, but you may wish to include them so that readers can more easily find the original passage.

> *revised* There is now wide agreement among linguists that the ease with which human children acquire their native tongues, under the conditions of a normal childhood, demonstrates an inborn capacity for language that is not shared by any other animals, not even those who are reared in comparable ways and given human language training (Deacon, 1997).

O *Paraphrasing*

Whereas a summary is a shorter version of its original, a paraphrase tends to be about the same length. However, paraphrases, like summaries, must reflect their sources accurately while using changed wording, and must include a citation. The original material's page number (or paragraph number for a nonpaginated online source) is not absolutely essential for a paraphrase, but APA suggests it be added as an aid to any reader who would like to refer to the original text. What follows is a paraphrase of the first sentence of the Deacon passage, which despite having a proper citation, falls short by being too close to the wording of the original (underlined).

needs checking　　Researchers in language have come to a consensus in the past few decades that the acquisition of language is innate; such contributions from knowledge contribute significantly to our ability to master such a complex system of communication (Deacon, 1997, p. 102).

Simply substituting synonyms for the words and phrases of the source, however, is not enough to avoid plagiarism. Even with its original wording, the next example also fails but for a very different reason: it follows the original's sentence structure, as illustrated in the interpolated copy below it.

needs checking　　Recently, linguists appear to have come to an agreement that speaking is an inborn skill, and that nothing but a substantial input from inborn cognition can account for the human capacity to acquire such a complicated means of expression (Deacon, 1997, p. 102).

　　　　　Recently (*over the last few decades*), linguists (*language researchers*) appear to have come to an agreement (*seem to have reached a consensus*) that speaking is an inborn skill (*that language is an innate ability*), and that nothing but a substantial input (*and that only a significant contribution*) from inborn cognition (*from innate knowledge*) can account for the human capacity (*can explain our ability*) to acquire such a complicated means of expression (*to learn such a complex communication system*) (Deacon, 1997, p. 102).

What follows is a good paraphrase of the passage's opening sentence; this paraphrase captures the sense of the original without echoing the details and shape of its language.

> *revised*   Linguists now broadly agree that children are born with the ability to learn language; in fact, the human capacity to acquire such a difficult skill cannot easily be accounted for in any other way (Deacon, 1997, p. 102).

O *Quoting Directly*

Unlike paraphrases and summaries, direct quotations must use the exact wording of the original. Because they involve importing outside words, quotations pose unique challenges. Quote too frequently, and you risk making your readers wonder why they are not reading your sources instead of your paper. Your essay should present something you want to say—informed and supported by properly documented sources, but forming a contribution that is yours alone. To that end, use secondary material to help you build a strong framework for your work, not to replace it. Quote sparingly, therefore; use your sources' exact wording only when it is important or particularly memorable.

To avoid misrepresenting your sources, be sure to quote accurately, and to avoid plagiarism, take care to indicate quotations as quotations, and cite them properly. If you use the author's name in a signal phrase, follow it with the date in parentheses, and be sure the verb of the phrase is in the past tense (*demonstrated*) or present perfect tense (*has demonstrated*). For all direct quotations, you must also include the page number (or paragraph number for a nonpaginated online source) of the original in your citation.

Below are two problematic quotations. The first does not show which words come directly from the source.

> *needs checking*   Deacon (1997) maintained that children enter the world predisposed to learn human languages (p. 102).

The second quotation fails to identify the source at all.

> *needs checking*   Many linguists have argued that "children enter the world predisposed to learn human languages."

The next example corrects both problems by naming the source and indicating clearly which words come directly from it.

> *revised*   Deacon (1997) maintained that "children enter the world predisposed to learn human languages" (p. 102).

◎ FORMATTING QUOTATIONS

There are two ways to signal an exact borrowing: by enclosing it in double quotation marks and by indenting it as a block of text. Which you should choose depends on the length and genre of the quotation and the style guide you are following.

⊙ Short Quotations

What counts as a short quotation differs among the various reference guides. In MLA style, "short" means up to four lines; in APA, up to forty words; and in Chicago Style, up to one hundred words. All the guides agree, however, that short quotations must be enclosed in double quotation marks, as in the examples below.

Short quotation, According to Deacon (1997), linguists agree that
full sentence: a human child's capacity to acquire language is inborn: "Without question, children enter the world predisposed to learn human languages" (p. 102).

Short quotation, According to Deacon (1997), linguists agree that
partial sentence: human "children enter the world predisposed to learn human languages" (p. 102).

⊙ Long Quotations

In APA style, longer quotations of forty words or more should be double-spaced and indented, as a block, one-half inch from the left margin. Do not include quotation marks; the indentation indicates that the words come exactly from the source. Note that indented quotations are often introduced with a full sentence followed by a colon.

> Deacon (1997) maintained that human beings are born with a unique cognitive capacity:
>
> > Without question, children enter the world predisposed to learn human languages. All normal children, raised in normal social environments, inevitably learn their local language, whereas other species, even when raised and taught in this same environment, do not. This demonstrates that human brains come into the world specially equipped for this function. (p. 102)

⊙ Quotations within Quotations

You may sometimes find, within the original passage you wish to quote, words already enclosed in double quotation marks. If your quotation is short, enclose it all in double quotation marks, and use single quotation marks for the embedded quotation.

> Deacon (1997) was firm in maintaining that human language differs from other communication systems in kind rather than degree: "Of no other natural form of communication is it legitimate to say that 'language is a more complicated version of that'" (p. 44).

If your quotation is long, keep the double quotation marks of the original. Note as well that in the example below, the source's use of italics (*simple*) is also faithfully reproduced.

> Deacon (1997) was firm in maintaining that human language differs from other communication systems in kind rather than degree:
>
> > Of no other natural form of communication is it legitimate to say that "language is a more complicated version of that." It is just as misleading to call other species' communication systems *simple* languages as it is to call them languages. In addition to asserting that a Procrustean mapping of one to the other is possible, the analogy ignores the sophistication and power of animals' non-linguistic communication, whose capabilities may also be without language parallels. (p. 44)

⊙ Adding to or Deleting from a Quotation

While it is important to use the original's exact wording in a quotation, it is allowable to modify a quotation somewhat, as long as the changes are clearly indicated and do not distort the meaning of the original. You may want to add to a quotation in order to clarify what would otherwise be puzzling or ambiguous to someone who does not know its context; put whatever you add in square brackets.

◉ *Using square brackets to add to a quotation*

Deacon (1997) concluded that children are born "specially equipped for this [language] function" (p. 102).

If you would like to streamline a quotation by omitting anything unnecessary to your point, insert an ellipsis (three spaced dots) to show that you've left material out.

◉ *Using an ellipsis to delete from a quotation*

When the quotation looks like a complete sentence but is actually part of a longer sentence, you should provide an ellipsis to show that there is more to the original than you are using.

Deacon (1997) concluded that "… children enter the world predisposed to learn human languages" (p. 102).

Note the square brackets example above; if the quotation is clearly a partial sentence, ellipses aren't necessary.

When the omitted material runs over a sentence boundary or constitutes a whole sentence or more, insert a period plus an ellipsis.

Deacon (1997) claimed that human children are born with a unique ability to acquire their native language: "Without question, children enter the world predisposed

to learn human languages…. [H]uman brains come into
the world specially equipped for this function" (p. 102).

Be sparing in modifying quotations; it is all right to have one
or two altered quotations in a paper, but if you find yourself
changing quotations often, or adding to and omitting from
one quotation more than once, reconsider quoting at all. A
paraphrase or summary is very often a more effective choice.

⊙ Integrating Quotations

Quotations must be worked smoothly and grammatically
into your sentences and paragraphs. Always, of course, mark
quotations as such, but for the purpose of integrating them
into your writing, treat them otherwise as if they were your
own words. The boundary between what you say and what
your source says should be grammatically seamless.

needs checking	Deacon (1997) pointed out, "whereas other species, even when raised and taught in this same environment, do not" (p. 102).
revised	According to Deacon (1997), while human children brought up under normal conditions acquire the language they are exposed to, "other species, even when raised and taught in this same environment, do not" (p. 102).

O *Avoiding "dumped" quotations*

Integrating quotations well also means providing a context
for them. Don't merely drop them into your paper or string
them together like beads on a necklace; make sure to introduce them by noting where the material comes from and
how it connects to whatever point you are making.

needs checking For many years, linguists have studied how human children acquire language. "Without question, children enter the world predisposed to learn human language" (Deacon, 1997, p. 102).

revised Most linguists studying how human children acquire language have come to share the conclusion articulated by Deacon (1997): "Without question, children enter the world predisposed to learn human language" (p. 102).

needs checking "Without question, children enter the world predisposed to learn human language" (Deacon, 1997, p. 102). "There is ... something special about human brains that enables us to do with ease what no other species can do even minimally without intense effort and remarkably insightful training" (Deacon, 1997, p. 103).

revised Deacon (1997) based his claim that we "enter the world predisposed to learn human language" on the fact that very young humans can "do with ease what no other species can do even minimally without intense effort and remarkably insightful training" (pp. 102–103).

O *Signal Phrases*

To leave no doubt in your readers' minds about which parts of your essay are yours and which come from elsewhere, identify the sources of your summaries, paraphrases, and quotations with signal phrases, as in the following examples.

- As Carter and Rosenthal (2011) demonstrated, ...
- According to Ming, Bartlett, and Koch (2014), ...

- In his latest article McGann (2015) advanced the view that …
- As Vieira (2020) observed, …
- Bonilla and Tillery (2020) have suggested that …
- Freschi (2004) was not alone in rejecting these claims, arguing that …
- Cabral, Chernovsky, and Morgan (2015) emphasized this point in their recent research: …
- Sayeed (2003) has maintained that …
- In a compelling article, Caxaj (2019) concluded that …
- In her later work, however, Hardy (2005) overturned previous results, suggesting that …

In order to help establish your paper's credibility, you may also find it useful at times to include in a signal phrase information that shows why readers should take the source seriously, as in the following example:

> In this lucid and groundbreaking work, psychologist and economist Daniel Kahneman (2011) described …

Here, the signal phrase mentions the author's professional credentials; it also points out the importance of his book, which is appropriate to do in the case of a work as famous as Kahneman's *Thinking Fast and Slow*.

Below is a fuller list of words and expressions that may be useful in the crafting of signal phrases:

according to _____,	agreed
acknowledged	allowed
added	argued
admitted	asserted
advanced	attested

believed	in the view of _____,
claimed	in the words of _____,
commented	insisted
compared	intimated
concluded	noted
confirmed	observed
contended	pointed out
declared	put it
demonstrated	reasoned
denied	refuted
disputed	rejected
emphasized	reported
endorsed	responded
found	suggested
granted	thought
illustrated	took issue with
implied	wrote

O *About In-Text Citations*

1. in-text citation: The APA system emphasizes the date of publication, which must appear within an in-text citation. Whenever a quotation is given, the page number, preceded by the abbreviation *p.*, must also be provided. Note that when two authors are mentioned in the body of the text, it is necessary to spell out the word "and":

- Rahman and Gilman (2020) argue that democratic participation needs to be "understood as a constant, sustained practice that outlives election cycles and stretches beyond voting or other formal, governmental channels for citizen imput" (p. 107).

APA Style

It is common to mention in the body of your text the surnames of authors that you are citing, as is done in the example above. If author names are not mentioned in the body of the text, however, they must be provided within the in-text citation. In the example below, note the comma between the names and date of publication.

- One analysis of democratic participation (Rahman & Gilman, 2020) emphasizes that civic engagement needs to be an ongoing process that "stretches beyond voting or other formal, governmental channels for citizen input" (p. 107).

If the reference does not involve a quotation (as it commonly does not in social science papers), only the date need be given as an in-text citation, provided that the author's name appears in the signal phrase. For paraphrases, APA encourages, though does not require, a page number reference as well. The in-text citation in this case must immediately follow the author's name:

- Rahman and Gilman (2020) argue that true democratic participation needs to be an ongoing process that extends beyond the process of formal voting (p. 107).

A citation such as this connects to a list of references at the end of the paper. In this case the entry under "References" at the end of the paper would be as follows:

- Rahman, K. S., & Gilman, H. R. (2020). *Civic power: Rebuilding American democracy in an era of crisis.* Cambridge University Press.

Notice here that the date of publication is again foregrounded, appearing immediately after the authors' names.

Notice that the formatting of titles must follow APA style; details follow below.

2. no signal phrase (or author not named in signal phrase): If the context does not make it clear who the author is, that information must be added to the in-text citation. Note that commas separate the author, the date, and the page number elements:

- Some political scientists are urging that democratic participation needs to be seen as an ongoing process that "stretches beyond voting or other formal, governmental channels for citizen input" (Rahman & Gilman, 2020, p. 107).

3. titles of stand-alone works: Stand-alone works are those that are published on their own rather than as part of another work. The titles of stand-alone works (e.g., journals, magazines, newspapers, books, and reports) should be in italics. Writers in the social and behavioral sciences do not normally put the titles of works in the bodies of their papers, but if you do include the title of a stand-alone work, all major words and all words of four letters or more should be capitalized. For book and report titles in the References list, however, capitalize only the first word of the title and subtitle (if any), plus any proper nouns. Journal, magazine, and newspaper titles in the list of References are exceptions; for these, capitalize all major words.

In-text:	Such issues are treated at length in *Ethical and Legal Issues in Nursing* (DeMarco et al., 2019).
References list:	DeMarco, J. P., Jones, G. E., & Daly, B. J. (2019). *Ethical and legal issues in nursing.* Broadview Press.

APA Style

4. titles of articles and chapters of books: The titles of these works, and anything else that is published as part of another work, are also not usually mentioned in the body of an essay, though if they are, they should be put in quotation marks, with all major words capitalized. In the References, however, titles of these works should *not* be put in quotation marks or italicized, and no words should be capitalized, with the exception of any proper nouns, and the first word in the title and the first in the subtitle, if any.

In-text:	In "End of Life and the Refusal of Treatment," the role of nurses in end-of-life care is analyzed in depth (DeMarco et al., 2019, pp. 139–191).
References list:	DeMarco, J. P., Jones, G. E., & Daly, B. J. (2019). End of life and the refusal of treatment. *Ethical and legal issues in nursing* (pp. 139–191). Broadview Press.

5. placing of in-text citations: When the author's name appears in a signal phrase, the in-text citation comes directly after the name. Otherwise, the citation follows the paraphrased or quoted material. If a quotation ends with punctuation other than a period or comma, then this should precede the end of the quotation, and a period or comma should still follow the parenthetical reference, if this is grammatically appropriate.

- The claim has been convincingly refuted by Ricks (2010), but it nevertheless continues to be put forward (Dendel, 2013).
- One of Berra's favorite coaching tips was that "ninety per cent of the game is half mental" (Adelman, 2007, p. 98).

- Adelman (2007) notes that Berra at one point said to his players, "You can observe a lot by watching!" (p. 98).
- Vieira (2020) considers the legitimacy of politicians claiming to represent silent constituencies.

6. citations when text is in parentheses: If a parenthetical reference occurs within text in parentheses, commas are used to set off elements of the reference.

- (See Figure 6.1 of Harrison, 2012, for data on transplant waiting lists.)

7. electronic source—page number unavailable: If online material is in PDF format, the page numbers are stable and may be cited as one would the pages of a printed source. Most online sources, however, lack page numbers altogether. In such cases you should provide a section or paragraph number if a reference is needed. For paragraphs, use the abbreviation "para."

- In a recent web posting a leading theorist has clearly stated that he finds such an approach "thoroughly objectionable" (Bhabha, 2012, para. 7).
- Carter and Zhaba (2009) describe this approach as "more reliable than that adopted by Perkins" (Method section, para. 2).

For ebooks, do not include location numbers, but provide the chapter, section, and/or paragraph numbers instead. If you are citing longer texts from electronic versions, chapter references may be more appropriate. For example, if the online Gutenberg edition of Darwin's *On the Origin of Species* were being cited, the citation would be as follows:

- Darwin refers to the core of his theory as an "ineluctable principle" (1856, Chapter 26).

Notice that *chapter* is capitalized and not abbreviated.

Students should be cautioned that online editions of older or classic works are often unreliable; typically there are far more typos and other errors in such versions than there are in print versions. It is often possible to exercise judgment about such matters, however. If, for example, you are not required to base your essay on a particular edition of Darwin's *Origin of Species* but may find your own, you will be far better off using the text you will find on the reputable Project Gutenberg site than you will using a text you might find on a site such as "Manybooks.com."

8. audiovisual works: Audio books, online lectures, You-Tube videos, TV shows, or movies should include a time stamp marking the relevant quotation instead of a page number.

- Adichie believes that people can and should act to create deep cultural change: "Culture does not make people; people make culture" (2012, 27.06–27.09).

9. two or more dates for a work: If you have consulted a re-issue of a work (whether in printed or electronic form), you should provide both the original date of publication and the date of the re-issue (the date of the version you are using).

- Emerson (1837/1909) asserted that America's "long apprenticeship to the learning of other lands" was "drawing to a close" (para. 1).

The relevant entry in the list of references would look like this:

- Emerson, R. W. (1909). *Essays and English traits*. P. F. Collier & Son. (Original work published 1837)

If you are citing work in a form that has been revised by the author, however, you should cite the date of the revised publication, not the original.

- In a preface to the latest edition of his classic work (2004), Watson discusses its genesis.

10. two authors: If there are two authors, both should be named either in the signal phrase or in the in-text citation. Use *and* in the signal phrase but *&* in parentheses.

- Chambliss and Best (2010) have argued that the nature of this research is practical as well as theoretical.
- Two distinguished scholars have argued that the nature of this research is practical as well as theoretical (Chambliss & Best, 2010).

11. three or more authors: In the body of the text and in the in-text citation, list the first author's name followed by "et al." (short for the Latin *et alia*: *and others*).

- Chambliss et al. (2011) have argued that the nature of this research is practical as well as theoretical.
- Four distinguished scholars have argued that the nature of this research is practical as well as theoretical (Chambliss et al., 2011).

If you are citing more than one work with similar groups of authors, you will need to write out more names to avoid confusion. If for example you are citing works with these two sets of authors:

> Haley, Caxaj, George, Hennebry (2020)
> Haley, Caxaj, Diaz, Cohen (2020)

You would cite them in-text as follows:

> (Haley, Caxaj, George, et al., 2020)
> (Haley, Caxaj, Diaz, et al., 2020)

12. organization as author: As you would with an individual human author, provide the name of an organization either in the body of your text or in a parenthetical citation. Recommended practice is to provide the full name of an organization on the first occasion, followed by an abbreviation, and then to use the abbreviation for subsequent references:

- Blindness has decreased markedly but at an uneven pace since the late 1800s (National Institute for the Blind [NIB], 2002).

13. author not given: If the author of the source is not given, it may be identified in the parenthetical reference by the title, which may be represented by a short form if the title is long.

- Confusion over voting reform is widespread ("Results of National Study," 2018).

14. date not given: Some sources, particularly electronic ones, do not provide a date of publication. Where this is the case, use the abbreviation *n.d.* for *no date*.

- Some still claim that evidence of global climate change is difficult to come by (Sanders, n.d.; Zimmerman, 2018).
- Sanders (n.d.) and Zimmerman (2018) still claim that evidence of global climate change is difficult to come by.

15. two or more works in the same citation: In this case, the works should appear in in-text citations in the same order they do in the list of references. If the works are by different authors, arrange the sources alphabetically by author's last name and separate the citations with a semicolon. If the works are by the same authors, arrange the sources by publication date. Add *a, b, c*, etc. after the year to distinguish works written by the same authors in the same year.

- Various studies have established a psychological link between fear and sexual arousal (Aikens et al., 1998; Looby & Cairns, 2008).
- Various studies appear to have established a psychological link between fear and sexual arousal (Looby & Cairns, 1999, 2002, 2005).
- Looby and Cairns (1999a, 1999b, 2002, 2005a, 2005b) have investigated extensively the link between fear and sexual arousal.

16. two or more authors with the same last name: If the References list includes two or more authors with the same last name, the in-text citation should supply an initial:

- One of the leading economists of the time advocated wage and price controls (H. Johnston, 1977).

17. works in a collection of readings or anthology: In the in-text citation for a work in an anthology or collection of readings, use the name of the author of the work, not that of the editor of the anthology. If the work was first published in the collection you have consulted, there is only the one date to cite. But if the work is reprinted in that collection after having first been published elsewhere, cite the date of the original publication and the date of the collection you have consulted, separating these dates with a slash. The following citation refers to an article by Ana S. Iltis that was reprinted in a collection of readings edited by Elisabeth Gedge and Wilfrid Waluchow.

- One of the essays in Gedge and Waluchow's collection argues that we should restrict, but not prohibit, placebo-controlled trials (Iltis, 2004/2012).

In your list of references, this work should be alphabetized under Iltis, the author of the piece you have consulted, not under Gedge.

The next example is a lecture by Georg Simmel first published in 1903, which a student consulted in an edited collection by Roberta Garner that was published in 2001.

- Simmel (1903/2001) argues that the "deepest problems of modern life derive from the claim of the individual to preserve the autonomy and individuality of his existence" (p. 141).

The reference list entry would look like this:

Simmel, G. (2001). The metropolis and mental life. In R. Garner (Ed.), *Social theory–Continuity and confrontation: A reader* (pp. 141–153). Broadview Press. (Original work published in 1903)

As you can see, in your reference list these works are listed under the authors of the pieces (Iltis or Simmel), not under the compilers, editors, or translators of the collection (Gedge & Waluchow or Garner). If you cite another work by a different author from the same anthology or book of readings, that should appear as a separate entry in your list of references—again, alphabetized under the author's name.

18. indirect source: If you are citing a source from a reference other than the source itself, you should use the phrase "as cited in" in your in-text citation.

- In de Beauvoir's famous phrase, "one is not born a woman, one becomes one" (as cited in Levey, 2001, para. 3).

In this case, the entry in your reference list would be for Levey, not de Beauvoir.

19. personal communications: These are any communications that cannot be found by your reader, such as emails, classroom lectures, messages on online discussion groups, text messages, unrecorded speeches, personal interviews, and conversations (among others). This type of communication should not be added to your list of references but documented only as an in-text citation. Provide the initials and surname of the person you communicated with as well as the date of communication.

- K. Montegna (personal communication, January 21, 2019) has expressed skepticism over this method's usefulness.

20. Indigenous traditional knowledge and oral traditions: APA guidelines suggest that before including Indigenous traditional knowledge in your paper, it should be confirmed to be both accurate and permitted—some Indigenous stories, for example, are to be told only at certain times and by certain people, and some are only to be told orally and are not meant to be printed. If the material you are citing can be found in a source discoverable by your readers, add it to your reference list following the formatting for the source type and cite in-text accordingly. If you spoke with an Indigenous person yourself or are citing materials that cannot be found by your readers, you can tailor the format for personal communications (see above) to create an in-text citation. In this case, give the person's full name and the Indigenous group to which they belong, as well as any other details that you think are important, followed by "personal communication" and the date or range of dates. It is also vital to communicate with the Indigenous person being cited, so they can confirm both that your citation is accurate and that they have agreed to be included in your work. Here is an example of how to format an in-text citation of a personal communication with an Indigenous writer:

- We spoke with Jeannette Armstrong (Sylix Nation, lives on the Penticton Indian Band Reserve, British Columbia, Canada, personal communication, June 1991) about her work as director of the En'owkin Centre ...

O *About References*

The list of references in APA style is an alphabetized listing of sources that appears at the end of an essay, article, or book. This list, entitled *References*, includes all the information necessary to identify and retrieve each of the sources you have cited, and only the works you have cited. Lists that include all the sources you have consulted are called *Bibliographies*, but these are not required by APA. The list of references should include only sources that can be accessed by your readers, and so it should not include personal communication, such as private letters, memos, e-mail messages, and telephone or personal conversations. Those should be cited only in your text (see the section above).

Entries should be ordered alphabetically by author surname, or, if there is no known author, by title. The first line of each entry should be flush with the left-hand margin, with all subsequent lines indented about one half inch. Double-space throughout the list of references.

The basic format for all entries consists of four major elements, all of which are somewhat flexible and can be customized to suit your source. The four elements (in the order they appear in your reference entry) are author, date, title, and source. Remember that one function of the list of references is to provide the information your readers need if they wish to locate your sources for themselves; APA allows any "non-routine" information that could assist in identifying the sources to be added in square brackets to any entry (e.g., [Sunday business section], [Film], [Interview with O. Sacks]).

In the References examples that follow, information about entries for electronic sources has been presented in an integrated fashion alongside information about referencing sources in other media, such as print, audiovisual, and so on.. Note that the DOI (Digital Object Identifier) or URL is the last element of your reference entry for digital sources, and a crucial one for readers when they want to use your reference to find the source. Include the DOI or URL as a hyperlink in your document, beginning "http://" or "https://". DOIs must be formatted "https://doi.org/xxxxx" (the "xxxxx" being the DOI number). Any articles with older DOI formatting should be reformatted to this new standard. This means that the label "DOI" is no longer needed before the link; it is also unnecessary to include the words "Accessed from" or "Retrieved from" before DOI and URL links. The only exception to this rule is if the material is unarchived and frequently updated—in this case you may want to add a retrieval date, as the content could differ if your reader seeks access at a later time. Copy and paste the DOI or URL directly into your References list; do not add line breaks, even if the hyperlink is moved onto its own line by your word-processing software. Do not add any other punctuation, including periods, as it may interfere with link functionality.

21. work with single author: For a work with one author the entry should begin with the last name, followed by a comma, and then the author's initials as applicable, followed by the date of publication in parentheses. Note that initials are generally used rather than first names, even when authors are identified by first name in the work itself. After the title of the work, add the publisher's name, leaving out abbreviations such as *Inc.* and *Co.* (but keeping *Press* and *Books*). If a DOI is available, APA requires that it be included, whether you are using the print or digital version; if there is no DOI, do not include one.

Filimowicz, M. (2022). *Digital totalitarianism: Algorithms and society.* Routledge.

22. two authors: List both authors by their last names and initials, separated by a comma and ampersand:

Caxaj, S., & Diaz, L. (2018). Migrant workers' (non)belonging in rural British Columbia, Canada: Storied experiences of marginal living. *International Journal of Migration, Health and Social Care, 14*(2), 208–220. https://doi.org/10.1108/ijmhsc-05-2017-0018

23. three to twenty authors: Last names should in all cases come first, followed by initials. Use commas to separate the authors' names, and use an ampersand rather than *and* before the last author. Note that the authors' names should appear in the order they are listed; sometimes this is not alphabetical.

Warne, R. T., Astle, M. C., & Hill, J. C. (2018). What do undergraduates learn about human intelligence? An analysis of introductory psychology textbooks. *Archives of Scientific Psychology, 6*(1), 32–50. https://doi.org/10.1037/arc0000038

APA Style

24. more than twenty authors: List the names of the first nineteen authors, add an ellipsis, and then give the last author's name.

> Akerboom, J., Chen, T., Wardill, T. J., Tian, L., Marvin, J. S., Mutlu, S., Calderón, N. C., Esposti, F., Borghuls, B. G., Sun, X. R., Gordus, A., Orger, M. B., Portugues, R., Engert, F., Macklin, J. J., Filosa, A., Aggarwal, A., Kerr, R. A., Takagi, R., ... Looger, L. L. (2012). Optimization of a GCaMP calcium indicator for neural activity imaging. *Journal of Neuroscience, 32*(40), 13819–13840. https://doi.org/10.1523/JNEUROSCI.2601-12.2012

25. works with an organization as author: If a work has been issued by a government body, a corporation, or some other organization and no author is identified, the entry should be listed by the name of the group. If this group is also the work's publisher, do not include the publisher in the source element of the citation.

> American Nurses Association. (2020). *Ethics Annual Report.* https://www.nursingworld.org/~4a0346/2020-center -for-ethics-and-human-rights-annual-report.pdf
>
> Broadview Press. (2019). *Annual report.* https://sec.report/ Document/0001398344-19-016555/
>
> Environment and Climate Change Canada. (2016). *Pan-Canadian framework on clean growth and climate change: Canada's plan to address climate change and grow the economy.* http://publications.gc.ca/pub?id=9.828774&sl=0

26. works with unknown author: When a work does not have an author, move the title to the author position in your citation. Only if the work is signed "Anonymous" do you begin the citation with "Anonymous" in the author position. Alphabetize the entry in your References list according to "Anonymous" (if applicable), or to the first important word in the title (ignoring articles such as "The," "A," and "An").

For in-text citations, once the title has been stated in full either in the narrative or in a parenthetical citation, you may from then on use an abbreviated version, italicized or in quotation marks, as appropriate. For example, the *Oxford English Dictionary* could be abbreviated as OED, and italicized in your in-text citation as (*OED*, 2019). The reference list entry would be as follows:

> *Oxford English Dictionary*. (2020). https://www.oed.com

27. two or more works by the same author: The author's name should appear for all entries. Entries should be ordered by year of publication, beginning with the earliest.

> Mouffe, C. (2019). *For a left populism*. Verso.
> Mouffe, C. (2020). *The return of the political*. Verso.

28. two or more works by the same author in the same year: If two or more cited works by the same author or group of authors have been published in the same year, see if they have more specific dates: if they do, list the works chronologically. If works are listed only by year, list them before the ones with a specific date. If two of the works have the same date, arrange these alphabetically according to the title and use letters to distinguish them: (2020a), (2020b), and so on.

> Employment and Social Development Canada. (2019a). *Temporary Foreign Worker Program 2012–2019*. https://open.canada.ca/data/en/dataset/76defa14 -473e-41e2-abfa-60021c4d934b
> Employment and Social Development Canada. (2019b). *What we heard: Primary agriculture review*. https://www. canada.ca/en/employment-social-development/services/ foreign-workers/reports/primary-agriculture.html

29. prefaces, introductions, forewords, afterwords: Cite these sections of a work as you would a chapter title:

> DeMarco, J. P., Jones, G. E., & Daly, B. J. (2019). Introduction. *Ethical and legal issues in nursing*. Broadview Press.

30. edited works: Entries for edited works include the abbreviation *Ed.* or *Eds.* The second example below is for a book with both an author and an editor; since the original work in this entry was published earlier than the present edition, that information is given in parentheses at the end.

> Armstrong, C. L., & Morrow, L. A. (Eds.). (2019). *Handbook of medical neuropsychology: Applications of cognitive neuroscience* (2nd ed.). Springer.
>
> Sapir, E. (1981). *Selected writings in language, culture, and personality*. D. G. Mandelbaum (Ed.). University of California Press. (Original work published 1949)

31. works with an author and a translator: The translator's name, along with the designation *Trans.*, is included in parentheses after the title; the original publication date is given in parentheses following the present edition's publication information.

> Jung, C. G. (2006). *The undiscovered self* (R. F. C. Hull, Trans.). Signet. (Original work published 1959)

32. selections from edited books and collections of readings: An article reprinted in an edited collection of readings should be listed as follows:

> Holmes, S., & Buchbinder, L. (2020). In a defunded health system, doctors and nurses suffer near-impossible conditions. In M. C. Schwartz (Ed.), *The ethics of pandemics* (pp. 25–27). Broadview Press.

33. selections from multivolume works:

> Truth, S. (2008). Speech delivered at the Akron, Ohio convention on women's rights, 1851. In A. Bailey, S. Brennan, W. Kymlicka, J. T. Levy, A. Sager, & C. Wolf (Eds.), *The Broadview anthology of social and political thought: Vol. 1. From Plato to Nietzsche* (pp. 964–965). Broadview Press. (Original work published 1851)

34. ebooks and audiobooks: If the ebook content is the same as an existing physical book, you do not need to specify which version you cited (APA style states that if a DOI is available, that information should be included whether you use the print or the electronic version). If the electronic version is different from the print, then you should specify that you are using the ebook version. Similarly, you do not need to state that you are using an audiobook version, unless it differs from the print version or you want to add narrator information.

> Atkins, J. W. (2013). *Cicero on politics and the limits of reason: The* Republic *and* Laws. Cambridge University Press. https://doi.org/10.1017/CBO9781107338722
>
> Herman, E. S., & Chomsky, N. (2017). *Manufacturing consent* (J. Pruden, Narr.) [Audiobook]. Random House. https://www.audible.ca/pd/Manufacturing -Consent-Audiobook/B072BSNQ9K (Original work published 1988)

35. periodical articles (with and without DOIs): Articles from journals, magazines, online platforms, and newspapers follow the same pattern of citation. Notice that article titles are not enclosed in quotation marks, and that both the periodical title and the volume number (if applicable) are in italics. If all issues of a given volume of a periodical begin with page 1, include the issue number as well, directly after the volume number, in parentheses and not italicized. Page ranges for periodicals should follow after a comma, be separated by an en dash, and close with a period. If there are discontinuous page numbers (in a print newspaper, for example), separate the page numbers with commas (for example 25–34, 45). The citation should finish with a period, unless it ends with a DOI or URL, in which case no period should be added. Include the DOI or URL as a hyperlink, beginning "http://" or "https://". DOIs must be formatted "https://doi.org/xxxxx" (the "xxxxx" being the DOI number). Note that if a DOI is available, APA asks that you add it to the citation, even if you consulted the print version.

Li, J., Osher, D. E., Hansen, H. A., & Saygin, Z. M. (2020). Innate connectivity patterns drive the development of the visual word form area. *Scientific Reports, 10*, Article 18039. https://doi.org/10.1038/s41598-020-75015-7

Luque, J. S., & Castañeda, H. (2012). Delivery of mobile clinic services to migrant and seasonal farmworkers: A review of practice models for community-academic partnerships. *Journal of Community Health, 38*(2), 397–407. https://doi.org/10.1007/s10900-012-9622-4

Pinquart, M., & Kauser, R. (2018). Do the associations of parenting styles with behavior problems and academic achievement vary by culture? Results from a meta-analysis. *Cultural Diversity and Ethnic Minority Psychology, 24*(1), 75–100. https://doi.org/10.1037/cdp0000149

Example from a periodical only available in print form (no DOI or URL):

Bowlin, B. (2019). Still alive, mostly. *The Fiddlehead, 281*, 47–48.

36. abstract of a periodical article: Cite as you would the journal article itself, adding *Abstract* in square brackets.

> Yang, C., Sharkey, J. D., Reed, L. A., Chen, C., & Dowdy, E. (2018). Bullying victimization and student engagement in elementary, middle, and high schools: Moderating role of school climate [Abstract]. *School Psychology Quarterly, 33*(1), 54–64. https://doi.org/10.1037/spq0000250

37. magazine articles: The basic principles are the same as for journal articles. Note that neither quotation marks nor italics are used for the titles of articles. If no author is identified, the title of the article should appear first. For monthly magazines, provide the month as well as the year; for magazines issued more frequently, give the day, month, and year.

> Aziza, S. (2020, October 30). For Persian Gulf migrant workers, the pandemic has amplified systemic discrimination. *The Nation.* https://www.thenation.com/article/world/migrants-coronavirus-persian-gulf/
>
> Dyer, A. (2012, November/December). The end of the world ... again. *SkyNews, 18*(4), 38–39.
>
> The rise of the yuan: Turning from green to red. (2012, October 20). *The Economist, 405*(42), 67–68.

38. newspaper articles: The basic principles to follow with newspaper articles or editorials are the same as with magazine articles (see above). Notice that if there is no letter assigned to a newspaper section, you should give the section's title in square brackets.

> Bennett, J. (2012, December 16). How to attack the gender pay gap? *The New York Times* [Sunday business section], 1, 6.
>
> Waldbieser, J. (2020, November 3). Escape the boredom trap. *New York Times.* https://www.nytimes.com/2020/

11/03/parenting/boredom-kids-pandemic.html
?searchResultPosition=7

39. reviews: Reviews of any type of media—books, TV shows, podcasts, films, albums—can be found in many different publications, including websites, newspapers, blogs, and magazines. Your reference should be formatted according to the citation format of the publication in which the review is found, with the name of the reviewer (if it has been provided) listed first, followed by the date and title of the review, and the information on the source itself, as follows:

> Semuels, A. (2020, January 14). Soon a robot will be writing this headline [Review of the book *A world without work: Technology, automation, and how we should respond*, by D. Susskind]. *New York Times.* https://www.nytimes.com/2020/01/14/books/review/a-world-without-work-daniel-susskind.html

40. reference work entries with an individual author: List by the author of the entry, if known; otherwise, list by the entry itself.

> Toole, B. A. (2017). Byron, (Augusta) Ada King, countess of Lovelace (1815–1852). In D. Cannadine (Ed.), *Oxford dictionary of national biography* (September 1, 2017 ed.). Oxford University Press. https://doi.org.10.1093/ref:odnb/37253

41. reference work entries with an organization as author: List the organization name in the author element of your citation. Note that if a reference work accessed online is continuously updated, you should use "n.d." as the publication year ("no date"). In this case, you should add a retrieval date in your citation.

American Psychological Association. (n.d.). Sample standard deviation. In *APA dictionary of psychology*. Retrieved
November 12, 2020, from https://dictionary.apa.org/
sample-standard-deviation

42. diagnostic manuals (DSM and ICD): If the publisher
and author are the same, you do not need to include the
publisher in your reference list citation.

American Psychiatric Association. (2013). *Diagnostic and
statistical manual of mental disorders* (5th ed.). https://
doi-org.10.1176/appi.books.9780890425596
World Health Organization. (2019). *International statistical
classification of diseases and related health problems* (11th
ed.). https://icd.who.int/browse11/l-m/en

Note that when citing these manuals in your text, they may
be abbreviated; it is also customary to create an in-text citation for a manual on the first mention of it:

- *Diagnostic and Statistical Manual of Mental Disorders*
  (5th ed.; DSM-5; American Psychiatric Association,
  2013)

After this first instance, it is not necessary to repeat citations
of these manuals in your paper (they can be referred to by
their abbreviations), unless you are quoting or paraphrasing,
in which case you should provide further in-text citations.

43. articles from databases: Some databases—such as
the Cochrane Database of Systematic Reviews and UpTo-
Date—make their articles available only within the databases. Format these citations as you would an article from a
periodical (see above).

Martin-McGill, K. J., Bresnahan, R., Levy, R. G., & Cooper,
P. N. (2020). Ketogenic diets for drug-resistant epilepsy.

Cochrane Database of Systematic Reviews. https://doi.
org/10.1002/14651858.CD001903.pub5

For the UpToDate database, include a retrieval date, because
these articles are continually edited, and the different versions are not archived:

> Kim, Y., & Gandhi, R. T. (2020). Coronavirus dis-
> ease 2019 (COVID-19): Management in hospital-
> ized adults. *UpToDate.* Retrieved November 17,
> 2020, from https://www.uptodate.com/contents/
> coronavirus-disease-2019-covid-19-management-in
> -hospitalized-adults?search=covid%2019%20treatment
> &source=covid19_landing&graphicRef=128045
> #graphicRef128045

**44. dissertations from a database, published and unpub-
lished**: Published theses and dissertations can be found on
databases such as ProQuest. For these references, the title of
the thesis or dissertation should be followed by a description ("Doctoral dissertation" or "Master's thesis," for example) and name of the institution that granted the degree in
square brackets.

> Porteny, T. (2019). *Improving migrant health policies and
> programs: From the normative to the positive* [Doctoral
> dissertation, Harvard University]. DASH: Digital Access
> to Scholarship at Harvard. http://nrs.harvard.edu/urn
> -3:HUL.InstRepos:42029506

If you are citing an unpublished thesis or dissertation, the
university granting the degree appears as the source element
rather than in square brackets after the title:

> Arthur, K. (2017). *We are having all kinds of fun: Fluidity
> in shoebox project* [Unpublished doctoral dissertation].
> University of Waterloo.

45. data sets: Entries for data sets in your references list should include the date of publication or of collection, as well as the version number. A retrieval date should only be included if the data are still being gathered. As with many of the APA bracketed descriptions, the one following the title is flexible, and you can use it to specify the kind of data you are citing (data set, code book, etc.).

> Statistics Canada. (2019). *Life expectancy, at birth and at age 65, by sex, three-year average, Canada, provinces, territories, health regions and peer groups* (Table 13100389) [Dataset]. https://open.canada.ca/data/en/dataset/00c99f50-4f07-4e8c-b61d-9e188a51ed82

46. software and reference apps: References to commonly used software and apps do not need to be cited in your paper unless you quote directly or paraphrase information from such a source. Below is an example of a reference list entry for information found on a reference app:

> Unbound Medicine, Inc. (2020). Anemia, in *Nursing Central* (Version 1.44) [Mobile app]. Apple App Store, https://apps.apple.com/ca/app/nursing-central/id300420397

47. films and video recordings: Begin entries for motion pictures with the name of the director, followed by the date of release, the film's title, the medium in square brackets, and the name of the studio. In most cases, the director of the film is stated in the author position of the citation; this element is flexible, however, and you can list the name of a host, producer, or composer if more appropriate.

> Attenborough, D. (Narrator). (2017). *Blue Planet II* [Nature Documentary Series]. BBC.
> Nolan, C. (Director). (2020). *Tenet* [Film]. Warner Bros; Syncopy.

48. episodes from television series: Entries for television show episodes should begin with the names of the writer and director, followed by the date, episode title, medium, series title, and production company's name. Identify the role, in parentheses, of each person listed. While the writer's and director's names are given in the example below, ·this element is flexible and you can include other relevant names if needed, along with their role descriptions.

> Lindelof, D., (Writer), Jefferson, C. (Writer), & Williams, S. (Director). (2019, November 24). This extraordinary being (Season1, Episode 6) [Television series episode]. In D. Lindelof (Executive Producer), *The Watchmen*. HBO; WarnerMedia.

49. TED Talks: If you are citing a TED Talk from the TED website, the author should be the speaker of the talk. If you are citing a version from YouTube, list the account owner as the author for ease of retrieval:

> Jauhar, S. (2019, July). How your emotions change the shape of your heart [Video]. TEDSummit. https://www.ted.com/talks/sandeep_jauhar_how_your_emotions_change_the_shape_of_your_heart?
>
> TED. (2019, October 5). Sandeep Jauhar: How emotions change the shape of your heart [Video]. YouTube. https://www.youtube.com/watch?v=mwoLhdHRt_0

50. YouTube and other streaming videos: As mentioned above, videos accessed on streaming services such as YouTube or Vimeo should have the person or organization who uploaded the video listed as author. If that person is simply a username, place the username in the author position; if the person's real name is known, place the name (inverted as usual) in the author position, followed by the username in square brackets.

Blank, D. (2009). Timelapse: Los Angeles wildfire [Video]. Vimeo. https://vimeo.com/6356422

University of Oxford. (2010, October 21). An introduction to general philosophy [Video lecture by Peter Millican]. YouTube. https://www.youtube.com/watch?v=hdCBGWcd4qw

51. podcasts: The host of the podcast should be listed as author, along with the role description in parentheses. The podcast should be specified as audio or visual in square brackets after the title. Add the URL when available—if you have accessed the podcast through an app, you may omit adding the URL.

Runciman, D. (Host). (2020, November 2). Are young people losing faith in democracy? (No. 285) [Audio podcast episode]. In *Talking Politics*. https://www.talkingpoliticspodcast.com/blog/2020/285-are-young-people-losing-faith-in-democracy

52. music recordings: Arrange an entry for a music recording as follows: give the writer's name, the copyright date of the piece of music, its title, the album title, the medium in square brackets, and the label name. If the piece is recorded by someone other than the writer, note that in square brackets after the piece's title. Add the recording date at the end of the entry if it differs from the copyright date. If the music is available only online, include a URL for ease of retrieval.

Cardi B. (2017). Bodak yellow [Song]. On *Invasion of Privacy* [Album]. Atlantic Records.

Chopin, F. (1996). *Nocturnes* [Recorded by Maria João Pires]. Deutsche Grammophon. (Original works written between 1827–1846)

Pass, J. (1988, February 3). Cheek to cheek [Song]. On *Blues for Fred* [Album; CD]. Pablo Records. (Original song by Irving Berlin published 1935)

53. recorded webinars: The following format should only be used for retrievable webinars; to cite unrecorded webinars, follow the formatting listed above for personal communications.

> Chodos, H., & Caron, L. (Guest speakers). (2019, January 31). *Best advice; Recovery-oriented mental health and addiction care in the patient's medical home* [Webinar]. Mental Health Commission of Canada. https://www.mentalhealthcommission.ca/English/media/4240

54. interviews: How you format an entry for an interview will depend on where it is located. If you watched or listened to a recording of the interview, use the format appropriate to the medium. The second example below is for an interview of Jane Goodall posted on YouTube. The first example is for an interview with Willie Nelson printed in a periodical. Here, the entry follows the format for a newspaper article, with the interviewer in the author position, and information about the interviewee in square brackets. Notice as well that, although the periodical is called a magazine, this publication goes by date only, not volume and issue number, and so the newspaper article format is the appropriate choice. These guidelines apply only to published interviews; unpublished interviews you have conducted yourself are considered private correspondence and should not be included in your References list.

> CBC News: The National. (2016, April 22). *Jane Goodall interview* [Video]. YouTube. https://www.youtube.com/watch?v=3h1UbYZV-IU
>
> Goldman, A. (2012, December 16). The silver-headed stranger [Interview with W. Nelson]. *New York Times Magazine*, p. 12.

55. blog posts: Start with the writer's name; then give the full date, entry title, blog title, and URL.

Accetti, C. I., & Oskian, G. (2020, November 17). What is a consultative referendum? The democratic legitimacy of popular consultations. *Political Science Now*. https://politicalsciencenow.com/what-is-a-consultative-referendum-the-democratic-legitimacy-of-popular-consultations/

56. Wikipedia article: Because Wikipedia pages can be revised by anyone, their content tends to change over time. In order for your readers to be able to access the same version of the article you are citing, use the archived version for your citation. To do this, go to the "View History" tab on the Wikipedia page and click on the date you accessed the article. The URL for that archived version is a permanent link that you can cite as the location in your reference. If the link is not labeled as permanent, include the retrieval date.

Behaviorism. (2020, August 4). In *Wikipedia*. https://en.wikipedia.org/w/index.php?title=Behaviorism&oldid=971230907

57. social media: When you use social media to discover content located elsewhere, cite the location of the original posting (for example if you find a news article via Twitter, cite the article itself, not the Tweet). Only create references for social media posts when you cite the content directly. If the author's real name is known, place the name (inverted as usual) in the author position, followed by the username in square brackets. If you only have the username, place it in the author position (including the symbol @, if applicable). Your reference should include all the non-standard spelling, capitalization, acronyms, and emojis that can be found in social media posts. If you cannot recreate an emoji in your word-processing software, include square bracketed descriptions "[smiling face with heart-eyes]" for example. A complete list of descriptions for the various emojis can be found at https://unicode.org/emoji/charts/emoji-list.html. The title of a social media post should be the text of the first 20 words. If there are any audiovisuals, include a square bracketed note to that effect after the title.

The following format for a Facebook post reference can be used for most social media platforms; further examples for Instagram and Twitter are included below.

58. Facebook posts:

> College of Nurses of Ontario. (2020, November 13). *What is "reflective practice"? Why do I need an action plan? Reflection should be part of a nurse's everyday routine* [Video]. Facebook. https://www.facebook.com/collegeofnurses/posts/2773432936208758
>
> Peltier, A. (2020, September 4). *For everyone who does work protecting the waters and the lands and to everyone we cross paths with, keep doing* [Link attached to notice of documentary screening featuring Peltier]. Facebook. https://www.facebook.com/Waterwarrior1/posts/901124333712126

59. Instagram photos or videos:

> Art Gallery of Ontario [@agotoronto]. (2020, August 23). *In the late 1950s and '60s, when artists felt pressure to live and work in the metropolitan centres of the world* [Photograph]. Instagram. https://www.instagram.com/p/CEPtIubAUmS/?utm_source=ig_web_copy_link

60. tweets: If the author's real name is known, provide it first, followed by the author's screen name in square brackets. If the author's real name cannot be determined, provide only the screen name, without the square brackets. Include only the date, not the time. Include the entire tweet.

Johnson Space Center [@NASA_Johnson]. (2020, November 17). Let the science begin! [Test tube emoji]. *Astronaut Kate Rubins has been conducting science experiments on the @Space_Station, and with NASA's SpaceX Crew-1* [Gif and link attached]. https://twitter.com/NASA_Johnson/status/1328751028242587649?s=20

61. other webpages and websites: In the case of websites and webpages that are not part of an overarching publication, create a reference for each page that you cite. If you are not quoting or paraphrasing the website in your text, but are discussing it generally, you do not need to create a reference for it—simply place the URL in parentheses as an in-text citation. If you are quoting or paraphrasing material from a webpage, and an author or editor is indicated, list by author; otherwise, list by title. If the source is undated or its content is likely to change, you should include the date on which you accessed the material. Use square brackets to include information that will help identify the source.

Fox, L. (2020, November 17). *Fate of the stimulus looks bleak as lawmakers turn attention to spending deadline*. CNN. https://www.cnn.com/2020/11/17/politics/stimulus -negotiations-latest-congress/index.html

World Health Organization. (2020, November 13). *WHO establishes council on the economics of health for all*. https:// www.who.int/news/item/13-11-2020-who-establishes -council-on-the-economics-of-health-for-all

62. visual works: When creating references for visual works such as paintings, maps, infographics, and photographs, include the medium in square brackets after the title.

63. work of art in a gallery or gallery website: Note that in this case the name of the gallery or museum, as well as the city, state, and country where it is located, are listed in the source element, in addition to the URL. If the work is not available on a website, omit the URL.

Paula, D. (2020). Liberata [Painting]. The Museum of Modern Art (MOMA), New York, NY, USA. https://www.moma.org/collection/works/415342 ?&on_view=1&with_images=1

64. stock images or clip art:

oksmith. (2020). *Doctor with mask #4* [Clip art]. Openclipart. https://openclipart.org/detail/325362/doctor -with-mask-4

65. infographics:

The Economist. (2020, November 13). *Against the clock: Performance of world chess champions and their opponents* [Infographic]. https://www.economist.com/graphic -detail/2020/11/13/the-queens-gambit-is-right-young -chess-stars-always-usurp-the-old

66. maps:

Pew Research Center. (2019, April 11). *Immigrant share in U.S. is lower than in many other countries* [Map]. https://www.pewresearch.org/fact-tank/2019/04/ 11/6-demographic-trends-shaping-the-u-s-and -the-world-in-2019/ft_19-01-31_foreignbornshare _immigrantshareinus_2-2/

67. photographs:

Adams, A. (1943). *Manzanar from Guard Tower, view west (Sierra Nevada in background), Manzanar Relocation Center, California* [Photograph]. Library of Congress. https://www.loc.gov/pictures/collection/manz/ item/2002695970/

68. PowerPoint slides, lecture notes, recorded Zoom lectures: If the slides, lecture notes, or recorded Zoom lectures you are citing are available online, create a reference such as the first example listed below. If the material is on a closed learning management system or intranet and your readers have access, include the name of the site and the URL for the login page in your reference (see the second example below). If your audience does *not* have access to the materials, cite these resources as personal communications (see above).

> University of British Columbia. (2011, November 24). *The social side of mobile health* [PowerPoint slides by D. Hooker]. SlideShare. https://www.slideshare.net/ubc/the-social-side-of-mobile-health-10314829

The following is a reference citation for a recorded Zoom class posted on an internal university learning management system:

> Ruddock, J. (2020, June 3). *Lecture 5: ENGL 234* [Archived recording of Zoom class]. Moodle. https://moodle.concordia.ca/moodle/course/view.php?id=125464

69. conference presentations: To cite a conference session that you attended in person, include the names of presenters in the author element, the date and title, and the name of the conference and location. If you accessed the discussion online, add the URL or DOI in the location element.

> Felher, B. (Chair), Cook, J., Johnson, P., & Lentschke, L. (Speakers). (2019, March 13–16). *Performing protest: Resistance rhetorics and the minoritarian response* [Panel]. Conference on College Composition and Communication, Pittsburgh, PA, United States.

Among the details to notice in this reference system:

- Where two or more works by the same author are included in References, they are ordered by date of publication.
- APA style prefers author initials rather than first names.
- Only the first words of titles and subtitles are capitalized, except for proper nouns.
- The date appears in parentheses near the beginning of each entry in References.
- The in-text citation comes directly after the name of the author or after the end quotation mark. Often, these citations fall just before the period or comma in the surrounding sentence.
- If an in-text citation occurs within text in parentheses, commas are used to set off elements of the reference.
- When a work has appeared in an edited collection, information on the editors must be included in the reference.
- Authors' first and last names are reversed; note the use of the ampersand (&) in place of *and* between author names.
- Translators should be included where appropriate in the References list.
- Publisher should be listed in References entries for print works.
- Months and publisher names are not abbreviated; the day of the month follows the name of the month.
- Online references include the date of publication or of last revision in parentheses immediately after the author's name. Note that, if a DOI or URL ends a reference entry, there is no period at the end of the entry.

○ *APA Style Sample Essay*

Following is a full sample of text with citations in APA style. The sample essay included here follows the APA guidelines for student papers, including the title page formatting that is recommended for students; your instructor may, of course, have specific requirements that you should also follow. Professional papers have different requirements under APA style. If you are submitting your paper for publication, consult with the publisher for formatting specifics, and see information on professional formatting on the APA website (https://apastyle.apa.org).

For student papers, include a title page, page numbers, your text, and a "References" page. Depending on the content of your paper, you may also include tables, figures, and appendices. APA guidelines suggest that student papers may omit a running head, author note, and abstract, unless your instructor requests that you include such elements.

1

Resistance to Vaccination: A Review of the Literature

Jeremy P. Yap

Psychology Department, Wagner College

PS 252: Health Psychology

Dr. J.B. Martin

February 25, 2021

top right-hand corner pagination begins with title page

include your course number and title, your instructor's name, and the due date for your paper on separate lines

title should be centered and bolded

Resistance to Vaccination: A Review of the Literature

Since the late 1990s, vaccination has become highly controversial. This paper will review the literature on the subject, with a particular focus on the vaccination of children, by posing and responding to three key questions:

1. How effective is the practice of vaccination—and how safe?

2. Why have vaccination rates declined?

3. What are the best ways to increase rates of vaccination?

This is an area in which medical science must engage with the research findings of social psychologists; there is an urgent need to find effective solutions. The problems are sufficiently complex, however, that it seems unlikely that any single approach will be sufficient to resolve them.

How Effective Is the Practice of Vaccination—and How Safe?

There is overwhelming evidence on a variety of fronts that vaccination is one of the great triumphs of modern medical science. Thanks to the spread of vaccination, smallpox and polio have been eliminated in most of the world. The Centers for Disease Control and Prevention (2020) reports that diseases such as measles, mumps, and rubella, for which a combined vaccine has for generations been routinely given to children, are almost unknown in areas where vaccination is near-universal. The example of measles is an instructive one. Before the practice of vaccination was introduced, measles infected several million children every year in the United States alone, and killed more than 500 annually. After vaccination became common practice, measles almost entirely disappeared in North America—until recently. Now

APA Style

3

it is a threat once again in the United States and Canada—and not a threat to be taken lightly. According to the World Health Organization (2020), measles still kills over 100,000 worldwide each year; for 2018 the figure was 142,300.

Evidence for the effectiveness of vaccination is very strong in the case of polio and smallpox, and in the case of "childhood diseases" such as measles and rubella. There is also strong evidence that vaccination against influenza has been successful in bringing about significantly reduced rates of infection (Atwell et al., 2019). Importantly, though, the success of vaccination depends in large part on so-called "herd immunity." So long as approximately 95% or thereabouts of a population have been vaccinated, the incidence of a disease catching on in that population is negligible. When vaccination rates dip below that level, however, the risk for those who have not been vaccinated increases dramatically. Despite this, some communities where vaccination is readily available nonetheless have vaccination rates dramatically below the percentage required for herd immunity. In California, for example, where a 2015 outbreak of measles has received wide attention, Maimuna et al. (2015) have estimated that in the relevant population clusters vaccination rates have dropped below 50%.

for citation of work with three or more authors use "et al."

What about the other side of the ledger? Have there been cases of patients suffering adverse effects after taking a vaccine? And if so, do the benefits of vaccination outweigh the risks? Here too the answers seem clear. Yes, there have been cases of adverse effects (notably, fever and

172 | APA STYLE SAMPLE ESSAY

4

allergic reactions for some individuals). But as Schmid (2017) and others
have concluded, these are rare, and on balance vastly outweighed by the
benefits of mass vaccination. Perhaps the broadest study of vaccines,
their effectiveness, and their occasional side effects was that conducted by
the Institute of Medicine (2011), which reviewed vaccines used against
chickenpox, influenza, hepatitis B, human papillomavirus, measles, mumps,
rubella, meningitis, and tetanus. Their conclusion was clear:

square
brackets
used for
a word
not in the
original
quotation

> Vaccines offer the promise of protection against a variety of
> infectious diseases ... [and] remain one of the greatest tools in the
> public health arsenal. Certainly, some vaccines result in adverse
> effects that must be acknowledged. But the latest evidence shows
> that few adverse effects are caused by the vaccines reviewed in this
> report. (p. 4)

Except in rare cases, then (as with certain individuals susceptible to severe
allergic reactions), the benefits of vaccines clearly far outweigh the risks.

centered
headings
for sections

Why Have Vaccination Rates Declined?

Near the end of the last century, British medical researcher Andrew
Wakefield and his colleagues (1998) published a study linking the
vaccination of children against diseases such as measles, mumps, and rubella
to increased incidence of gastrointestinal disease, and also to increased
incidence of "developmental regression"—notably, autism. The study
appeared in *The Lancet*, one of the world's leading medical journals, and
had a major impact—but an entirely unfortunate one. News of the study's

5

findings spread widely, with thousands of articles in the popular press in 2001 and 2002 questioning the safety of vaccination. Parents whose children suffered from autism started to blame vaccination, and many of them launched lawsuits.

It was not until six years later that serious doubts were publicly raised. Investigative journalist Brian Deer (2004) revealed that Wakefield's study was compromised by a serious conflict of interest; he had received financial compensation from parties intending to sue vaccine manufacturers before he embarked on the research. And, as was gradually discovered, the research itself had been fabricated. In 2010 *The Lancet* finally retracted the 1998 article, and Wakefield himself was censured. By that time, a very great deal of damage had been done; public confidence in vaccines had dropped precipitously.

Fabricated research results are not the sole cause of the lack of confidence in vaccination that many continue to express. To some extent, confidence in vaccination among the general public has always been shaky. The very nature of vaccination—giving the patient a very small, modified dose of an illness in order to prevent further harm—seems counterintuitive to many. As Brendan Nyhan observed in an interview with Julia Belluz (2015), "people have always been suspicious of vaccines. There has always been an instinctive response to the idea of using a disease to protect yourself against the disease. It gives people the heebie jeebies" (para. 8). In a meta-analysis, Atwell et al. (2019) report that humans are far more

provide paragraph number when page numbers are unavailable

APA Style

likely to get vaccinated when they believe the disease in question to pose a serious threat—a finding which should not come as surprising, and which explains why doubts about vaccines have found fertile ground in places where the vaccines themselves have largely or entirely succeeded. As Jerome Groopman (2015) has observed, "we no longer see children stricken with polio in wheelchairs, or hear of those suffocating from diphtheria, of babies born to mothers with rubella whose eyes are clouded by cataracts and hearts deformed" (p. 30). If one continually sees people suffering from such diseases, one is likely to be far more aware of their dangers than is the case in nations where vaccination has succeeded in reducing their incidence to zero or near-zero.

When doubts have been raised and scandals have arisen, the media have too often not been as responsible as one would wish. On the one hand, as discussed by Nelson (2014), Jennings (2019) and others, some media outlets have tacitly encouraged scientifically irresponsible statements by taking an "impartial" approach to the facts, reporting the claims of anti-vaccination activists with no scientific credentials and of reputable scientific authorities as if they had equal authority. Other media outlets, however, have sometimes swung too far in the other direction, adopting a supercilious or contemptuous tone towards those who have doubts about vaccination. Much as it is important to spread factual information as to the dangers of allowing one's children to remain unvaccinated, it is counterproductive to present information in a tone that is disrespectful of the audience one is hoping to persuade. As Angelina Chapin (2015) has pointed out, when

> people's beliefs contradict science, there's an obvious temptation
> to cut them down. But we should be more careful with how we
> deliver our arguments. On a policy level, messaging should come
> from people that communities trust, such as doctors or religious
> leaders. At the dinner table or on Facebook, try a little empathy.
> It will help the medicine go down and the immunization rates go
> up. (para. 12)

The attitudes with which we approach these discussions, in short, can make
a world of difference.

Interestingly, studies such as that of Maimuna et al. (2015) suggest
that those with high levels of education are at least as likely as those with
less education to be anti-vaccination. One important factor in the social
psychology of attitudes towards vaccination that does seem to have had
an impact (albeit a negative one), has been the degree to which the issue
has become charged with ideological content. Those who are generally
suspicious of government and/or of modern science have been slow to accept
the overwhelming weight of evidence in support of vaccination. That should
perhaps not be surprising; as Kraft et al. (2015) and others have reported, to
the extent that beliefs about factual matters are intertwined with ideology,
our minds become immunized against information in the other direction,
even when that information is of a purely factual nature. Moreover, this is a
"tendency that appears to be evident among liberals and conservatives alike"

acceptable
to include
first name
in a signal
phrase

APA Style

(p. 121). When they are colored by ideology—and by emotion—our beliefs as to the facts of the matter are highly resistant to change.

What Are the Best Ways to Increase the Rates of Vaccination?

Clearly it is important for health care workers, educators, and those in the media to inform themselves of the facts and to spread this information. But simply informing the public of the facts is evidently insufficient to change behavior. Several studies have found that parents who have been fully informed of the scientific background are no more likely to vaccinate their children—and in some cases are *less* likely (Callaghan et al., 2019; Nyhan et al., 2014).

Just as important as the facts themselves, it seems, is the way they are reported to patients. The attitudes expressed by health care workers to patients play a key role. Though the vast majority of health care workers accept the evidence regarding vaccination, they have become aware that it is a hot-button issue and—not wanting to be insensitive to patients' concerns—have sometimes not been clear and emphatic about the dangers of not vaccinating. If health care workers ask parents if they "believe in" vaccinating their children, their phrasing is likely to provide support to the views of those patients who think the science about vaccinations to be uncertain. Conversely, an attitude that remains friendly while taking the facts as a given may be more helpful. There have been numerous studies on the degree to which it may help to frame information positively to patients (Anderson et al., 2020; Thomson et al., 2018; and Wegwartha et al., 2014).

9

Though these have not been entirely conclusive, it is hard to imagine that it is not preferable to present facts in a tone that will encourage others to appreciate them, and to act accordingly. Angelina Chapin's common-sense advice on this point (quoted above) rings true.

It may well be, however, that adopting the right tone with patients and in media reports will not be enough; regulatory and/or legislative changes may be required as well in some jurisdictions. It is important to note that the United States as a whole has not suffered any steep decline in vaccination rates; to a large extent the problem is associated with jurisdictions that make it easy for parents to opt out of vaccinations for their children. In contrast, where vaccination is the strong "default position"—mandatory for children with few possible exemptions—vaccination rates in recent years have tended to remain at well over 90%. As Margaret Talbot (2015) has observed of the United States,

> the highest vaccination rate in the country is in
> Mississippi, a state with an otherwise dismal set of
> health statistics. It allows people to opt out of vaccines
> only for medical reasons—not for religious or personal ones.
> States that make it easier not to vaccinate have
> higher rates of infectious diseases. (pp. 19–20)

quotation of more than 40 words is indented 0.5 inches from left margin

Is the answer, then, simply to pass stricter laws in jurisdictions that currently have loose ones? Much as such action may be desirable, given current levels of resistance to vaccination of children, it is questionable whether efforts to

APA Style

make the practice mandatory would be successful in many areas—and they would be sure to inflame passions on all sides.

The experience of the European Union suggests that it may not always be necessary to make vaccination mandatory. Vaccination rates are high throughout Europe, even though only 14 of the 29 countries in the EU have any mandatory vaccinations (Haverkate et al., 2012). In the remainder, vaccination is recommended rather than required. There is some evidence that in North America, too, non-compulsory strategies can in certain circumstances be as effective as compulsion in raising vaccination rates (El-Amin et al., 2012). Again, the strength with which a recommendation is put forward can make a world of difference to the degree to which that recommendation is followed. If parents are simply informed that vaccination is recommended and that they may vaccinate their children against measles if they wish at such and such a time and place, the uptake rate is likely to be low. If parents are informed that a medical ordinance specifies that children should be vaccinated against measles, and that low vaccination rates put all children at risk, the uptake rate will surely be much higher.

There is a widespread tendency to presume that Americans will be more likely to resist government "intrusions" into citizens' lives than will Canadians. In the case of attitudes towards vaccination, however, it is not at all clear that the presumption is correct. Whereas every American state has at least some requirement (albeit often weakened by "personal belief" exemptions) that children be vaccinated before attending school, only a

11

minority of Canadian provinces have such regulations (Walkinshaw, 2011).

Whatever approaches are taken in each jurisdiction, it will be essential that attention be paid not only to the medical and biological facts, but also to laws and regulations—and to social psychology.

list of
references
begins
on a new
page

list of references alphabetized by author's last name

References

Anderson, M. G., Ballinger, E. A., Benjamin, D., Frenkel, L. D., Hinnant Jr., C. W., & Zucker, K. W. (2020). A clinical perspective of the U.S. anti-vaccination epidemic: Considering marginal costs and benefits, CDC best practices guidelines, free riders, and herd immunity. *Vaccine*, *38*(50), 7877–7879. https://doi.org/10.1016/j.vaccine.2020.10.068

Atwell, K., Dube, E., Gagneur, A., Omer, S. B., & Suggs, L. S. (2019). Vaccine acceptance: Science, policy, and practice in a "post-fact" world. *Vaccine*, *37*(5), 677–682. https://doi.org/10.1016/j.vaccine.2018.12.014

Belluz, J. (2015, February 7). Debunking vaccine junk science won't change people's minds. Here's what will [Interview with B. Nyhan]. *Vox*. http://www.vox.com/2015/2/7/7993289/vaccine-beliefs

Callaghan, T., Motta, M., Sylvester, S., Trujillo, K., & Blackburn, C. C. (2019). Parent psychology and the decision to delay childhood vaccination. *Social Science & Medicine*, *238*(112407). https://doi.org/10.1016/j.socscimed.2019.112407

Centers for Disease Control and Prevention. (2020, November 5). *Measles History*. https://www.cdc.gov/measles/about/history.html

Chapin, A. (2015, February 13). How to talk to anti-vaxxers. *Ottawa Citizen*. http://ottawacitizen.com/opinion/columnists/how-to-talk-to-anti-vaxxers

Deer, B. (2004, February 22). Revealed: MMR research scandal. *The Sunday Times* (London). http://www.thesundaytimes.co.uk/sto/

author initials used—not first names

APA Style

13

El-Amin, A. N., Parra, M. T., Kim-Farley, R., & Fielding, J. E. (2012). Ethical issues concerning vaccination requirements. *Public Health Reviews, 34*(1), 1–20. http://www.publichealthreviews.eu/upload/pdf_files/11/00_El_Amin.pdf

Groopman, J. (2015, March 5). There's no way out of it [Review of the book *On immunity: An introduction*]. *The New York Review of Books*, 29–31.

Haverkate, M., D'Ancona, F., Giambi, C., Johansen, K., Lopalco, P. L., Cozza, V., & Appelgren, E. (2012, May). Mandatory and recommended vaccination in the EU, Iceland and Norway: Results of the VENICE 2010 survey on the ways of implementing national vaccination programmes. *Eurosurveillance, 17*(22), 31. http://www.eurosurveillance.org/ViewArticle.aspx?ArticleId=20183

Institute of Medicine. (2011, August 25). Adverse effects of vaccines: Evidence and causality [Report brief]. http://www.iom.edu/Reports/2011/Adverse-Effects-of-Vaccines-Evidence-and-Causality.aspx

Jennings, F. J., & Russell, F. M. (2019). Civility, credibility, and health information: The impact of uncivil comments and source credibility on attitudes about vaccines. *Public Understanding of Science, 28*(4), 417–432. https://doi.org/10.1177/0963662519837901

Kraft, P. W., Lodge, M., & Taber, C. S. (2015, March). Why people "don't trust the evidence": Motivated reasoning and scientific beliefs. *Annals of the American Academy of Political and Social Science, 658*(1), 121–133.

provide URL for web-sourced material when DOI not available

https://doi.org/10.1177/0002716214554758

Maimuna, S., Majumder, M. P. H., Cohn, E. L., Sumiko, R., Mekaru, D. V. M., Huston, J. E., & Brownstein, J. S. (2015, March 16). Substandard vaccination compliance and the 2015 measles outbreak [Research Letter]. *JAMA Pediatrics, 169*(5), 494–495. https://doi.org/10.1001/jamapediatrics.2015.0384

Nelson, R. (2014, October). The reporting of health information in the media. *American Journal of Nursing, 114*(10), 19–20. https://doi.org/10.1097/01.NAJ.0000454842.04985.c6

Nyhan, B., Reifler, J., Richey, S., & Freed, G. L. (2014, April 1). Effective messages in vaccine promotion: A randomized trial. *Pediatrics, 133*(4), e835–e842. https://doi.org/10.1542/peds.2013-2365

Schmid, P., Rauber, D., Betsch, C., Lidolt, G., & Denker, M. (2017). Barriers of influenza vaccination intention and behavior: A systematic review of influenza vaccine hesitancy, 2005–2016. *PLoS ONE, 12*(1). https://doi.org/10.1371/journal.pone.0170550

Talbot, M. (2015, February 16). Not immune. *The New Yorker, 91*(1), 19–20.

Thomson, A., Vallée-Tourangeau, G., & Suggs, L. S. (2018). Strategies to increase vaccine acceptance and uptake: From behavioral insights to context-specific, culturally-appropriate, evidence-based communications and interventions. *Vaccine, 36*(44), 6457–6458. https://doi.org/10.1016/j.vaccine.2018.08.031

all materials that have a DOI available must include the DOI in the reference entry, even if you accessed a print version

APA Style

15

Wakefield, A. J., Murch, S. H., Anthony, A., Linnel, J., Casson, D. M., Malik, M., Berelowitz, M., Dhillon, A. P., Thomson, M. A., Harvey, P., Valentine, A., Davies, S. E., & Walker Smith, J. A. (1998). Ileal-lymphoidnodular hyperplasia, non-specific colitis, and pervasive developmental disorder in children. *Lancet, 351*, 637–641. https://doi.org/10.1016/S0140-6736(97)11096-0 (Retraction published 2010, *Lancet, 375*, p. 445)

Walkinshaw, E. (2011, November 8). Mandatory vaccinations: The international landscape. *Canadian Medical Association Journal, 183*(16), e1167–e1168. https://doi.org/10.1503/cmaj.109-3993

Wegwartha, O., Kurzenhäuser-Carstens, S., & Gigerenzera, G. (2014, March 10). Overcoming the knowledge–behaviour gap: The effect of evidence-based HPV vaccination leaflets on understanding, intention, and actual vaccination decision. *Science Direct: Vaccine, 32*(12), 1388–1393. https://doi.org/10.1016/j.vaccine.2013.12.038

World Health Organization. (2020, October 27). *Measles (Immunization, Vaccines and Biologicals).* http://www.who.int/immunization/monitoring_surveillance/burden/vpd/surveillance_type/active/measles/en/

paste DOIs or URLs into your citation; do not add punctuation

Chicago Style

About Chicago Style   187
  1.   notes   188
  2.   titles: italics/quotation marks   189
  3.   multiple references to the same work   190
  4.   page number or date unavailable   190
  5.   two or more dates for a work   192
  6.   two or three authors   193
  7.   four or more authors   193
  8.   organization as author/reference work/government
       document   193
  9.   works from a collection of readings or anthology   195
 10.   indirect source   196
 11.   two or more works by the same author   196
 12.   edited works   196
 13.   translated works   197
 14.   e-books   197
 15.   magazine articles   198
 16.   newspaper articles   199
 17.   journal articles   199
 18.   films and video recordings   200
 19.   television broadcasts   201
 20.   sound recordings   201
 21.   interviews and personal communications   202
 22.   book reviews   203
 23.   blog posts   203
 24.   websites   203
 25.   online videos   204
 26.   tweets   204

Chicago Style Sample   206

◎ Chicago Style

○ *About Chicago Style*

The University of Chicago's massively comprehensive *Chicago Manual of Style* (17th edition, 2017) provides full information on two documentation systems: an author-date system of citation that is similar to APA style, and a traditional foot- or endnoting system. The latter, which this book refers to as Chicago Style, and which is often used in the history and philosophy disciplines, is outlined below. This chapter also includes, at the end, a short essay excerpt using Chicago Style documentation. Full sample essays in Chicago Style are available on the Broadview website. Go to sites.broadviewpress.com/writing/. You can also find additional information at Chicago Style's online site (www.chicagomanualofstyle.org).

In the pages that follow, information about electronic sources has been presented in an integrated fashion, with information about referencing hard copies of print sources presented alongside information about referencing online versions. General guidelines covering entries for online sources are as follows. Begin each note and bibliography entry for an electronic source as you would for a non-electronic source, including all relevant publication information that the source makes available. Then provide either the website's URL, followed by the usual end punctuation for the note or entry, or, if available, the source's digital object identifier (DOI): a string of numbers, letters, and punctuation, beginning with *10*, usually located on the first or copyright page. If both a URL and DOI

Chicago Style

are available, provide only the latter; DOIs are preferred because they are stable links to sources, whereas URLs are often not permanent. If you need to break a URL or DOI over two or more lines, do not insert any hyphens at the break point; instead, break after a colon or double slash or before other marks of punctuation. Note that Chicago Style does not put angle brackets around URLs. Except when there is no publication or modification date available, Chicago Style does not require the addition of access dates for online material, but your instructors may wish you to include them. If so, put them before the URL or DOI, after the word *accessed*.

1. notes: The basic principle of Chicago Style is to create a note each time one cites a source. The note can appear at the foot of the page on which the citation is made, or it can be part of a separate list, titled *Notes*, situated at the end of the essay and before the bibliography. For both foot- and endnotes, a superscript number at the end of the clause in which the reference appears points to the relevant note:

- Levy and Mole suggest that the emotional attachment some people feel for print books is "historically and culturally constructed, and it could be constructed differently in the future."[1]

The superscript number [1] here is linked to the information provided where the same number appears at either the foot of the page or in the list of notes at the end of the main text of the paper:

1. Michelle Levy and Tom Mole, *The Broadview Introduction to Book History* (Peterborough, ON: Broadview Press, 2017), 138.

Notice that the author's name is in the normal order, elements of the note are separated by commas, publication information is in parentheses, and the first line of the note is indented. The note ends with a page number for the citation.

In addition, all works cited, as well as works that have been consulted but are not cited in the body of your essay, must be included in an alphabetically arranged list, titled *Bibliography*, that appears at the end of the essay. The entry there would in this case be as follows:

> Levy, Michelle, and Tom Mole. *The Broadview Introduction to Book History*. Peterborough, ON: Broadview Press, 2017.

In the entry in the bibliography, notice that the first author's name is inverted, elements of the entry are separated by periods, and no parentheses are placed around the publication information. Also, the entry is given a hanging indent: the first line is flush with the left-hand margin, and subsequent lines are indented. Notice as well that the province or state of publication is included in both notes and bibliography entries if the city of publication is not widely known.

In the various examples that follow, formats for notes and bibliography entries for each kind of source are shown together.

2. titles: italics/quotation marks: Notice in the above example that the title is in italics. Titles of short works (such as articles, poems, and short stories) should be put in quotation marks. In all titles key words should be capitalized. For more details, see the Title of Source section in the chapter on MLA documentation above (pp. 48–50).

3. multiple references to the same work: For later notes referencing an already-cited source, use the author's last name, title (in shortened form if it is over four words long), and page number only.

> 1. Levy and Mole, *Broadview Introduction to Book History*, 154.

If successive references are to the same work, you may omit the title of the work just cited, in order to avoid repetition.[*]

> 1. Sean Carver, "The Economic Foundations for Unrest in East Timor, 1970–1995," *Journal of Economic History* 21, no. 2 (2011): 103.
> 2. Carver, 109.
> 3. Carver, 111.
> 4. Jennifer Riley, "East Timor in the Pre-Independence Years," *Asian History Online* 11, no. 4 (2012): par. 18, http://www.aho.ubc.edu/prs/text-only/issue.45/16.3jr.txt.
> 5. Riley, par. 24.

Carver, Sean. "The Economic Foundations for Unrest in East Timor, 1970–1995." *Journal of Economic History* 21, no. 2 (2011): 100–21.

Riley, Jennifer. "East Timor in the Pre-Independence Years." *Asian History Online* 11, no. 4 (2012). http://www.aho .ubc.edu/prs/text-only/issue.45/16.3jr.txt.

4. page number or date unavailable: If an internet document is in PDF format, the page numbers are stable and

---

[*] This recommendation represents a change from previous editions, which had recommended using *ibid.* (an abbreviation of the Latin *ibidem*, meaning *in the same place*) for successive references. The 17th edition discourages the use of *ibid.*

may be cited in the same way that one would the pages of a printed book or journal article. Many internet pages are unstable, however, and many more lack page numbers. Instead, provide a section number, paragraph number, or other identifier if available.

2. Hanif Bhabha, "Family Life in 1840s Virginia," *Southern History Web Archives* 45, no. 3 (2013): par. 14, accessed March 3, 2021, http://shweb.ut.edu/history/american.nineteenthc/bhabha.html.

Bhabha, Hanif. "Family Life in 1840s Virginia." *Southern History Web Archives* 45, no. 3 (2013). Accessed March 3, 2021. http://shweb.ut.edu/history/american.nineteenthc/bhabha.html.

If you are citing longer texts from electronic versions, and counting paragraph numbers is impracticable, chapter references may be more appropriate. For example, if the online Gutenberg edition of Darwin's *On the Origin of Species* were being cited, the citation would be as follows:

- Darwin refers to the core of his theory as an "ineluctable principle."[1]

1. Charles Darwin, *On the Origin of Species* (1856; Project Gutenberg, 2001), chap. 26, http://www.gutenberg.darwin.origin.frrp.ch26.html.

Darwin, Charles. *On the Origin of Species*. 1856. Project Gutenberg, 2001. http://www.gutenberg.darwin.origin.frrp.ch26.html.

Students should be cautioned that online editions of older or classic works are often unreliable; typically there are far more typos and other errors in online versions of literary texts than there are in print versions. It is often possible to exercise judgment about such matters, however. If, for example, you are not required to base your essay on a particular edition of Darwin's *Origin of Species* but may find your own, you will be far better off using the text you will find on the reputable Project Gutenberg site than you will using a text you might find on a site such as "Manybooks. com."

When there is no date for a source, include *n.d.*, as in the first example below. When there is no date for an online source, include your access date.

    1. Thomas Gray, *Gray's Letters*, vol. 1 (London: John Sharpe, n.d.), 60.

    2. Don LePan, *Skyscraper Art*, accessed February 10, 2020, http://www.donlepan.com/Skyscraper_Art.html.

Gray, Thomas. *Gray's Letters*. Vol. 1. London: John Sharpe, n.d.

LePan, Don. *Skyscraper Art*. Accessed February 10, 2020. http://www.donlepan.com/Skyscraper_Art.html.

5. two or more dates for a work: Note that in the Darwin example above both the date of the original publication and the date of the modern edition are provided. If you are citing work in a form that has been revised by the author, however, you should cite the date of the revised publication, not the original, and use the abbreviation *rev. ed.* to indicate that the work has been revised.

    1. Robert Mutti, *Making Up Your Mind*, rev. ed. (Peterborough, ON: Broadview Press, 2014), 150.

Mutti, Robert. *Making Up Your Mind*. Rev. ed. Peterborough, ON: Broadview Press, 2014.

6. two or three authors: If there are two or three authors, they should be identified as follows in the footnote and in the bibliography. Pay attention to where commas do and do not appear, and note that in the bibliography entry, only the first author's name is inverted. Put the names of the authors in the order in which they appear in the work itself.

> 1. Joerg Fingerhut and Jesse J. Prinz, "Aesthetic Emotions Reconsidered," *The Monist* 103, no. 2 (April 2020): 223, https://doi.org/10.1093/monist/onz037.

> Fingerhut, Joerg, and Jesse J. Prinz. "Aesthetic Emotions Reconsidered." *The Monist* 103, no. 2 (April 2020): 223–29. https://doi.org/10.1093/monist/onz037.

7. four or more authors: In the footnote name only the first author, and use the phrase *et al.*, an abbreviation of the Latin *et alia*, meaning *and others*. In the bibliography name all authors, as below:

> 11. Victoria Fromkin et al., *An Introduction to Language*, 4th Canadian ed. (Toronto: Nelson, 2010), 113.

> Fromkin, Victoria, Robert Rodman, Nina Hyams, and Kirsten M. Hummel. *An Introduction to Language*. 4th Canadian ed. Toronto: Nelson, 2010.

8. organization as author/reference work/government document: Identify by the organization if known, and otherwise by the title of the work. Unsigned newspaper articles or dictionary and encyclopedia entries are usually not listed in the bibliography. In notes, unsigned dictionary or encyclopedia entries are identified by the title of the reference work, e.g., Wikipedia, and unsigned newspaper articles are listed by the title of the article.

6. Major League Baseball, *2021 Regular Season Standings*, accessed June 9, 2021, https://www.mlb.com/standings.

7. "Argentina's President Calls on UK Prime Minister to Relinquish Control of Falkland Islands," *Vancouver Sun*, January 3, 2013, A9.

8. Broadview Press, "Broadview's 2020 Recycled Paper Usage and Charitable Donations," accessed May 3, 2021, https://broadviewpress.com/broadviews-2020-recycled-paper-usage-and-charitable-donations/.

9. Commonwealth Corporation of Massachusetts, *Resources for Individuals & Communities in Response to Coronavirus (COVID-19)*, 2020, accessed January 12, 2021, https://archives.lib.state.ma.us/bitstream/handle/2452/831037/on1178881472.pdf?sequence=1&isAllowed=y.

10. Wikipedia, s.v. "Mary Wollstonecraft," last modified May 19, 2021, 11:46, https://en.wikipedia.org/w/index.php?title=Mary_Wollstonecraft&oldid=1023975388.

11. *OED Online*, s.v. "aesthetic, n.1," last modified March 2021, accessed May 25, 2021, https://www-oed-com./view/Entry/3237?rskey=49BHJn&result=1&isAdvanced=false.

The following are the bibliography entries for the preceding notes (notice that, because unsigned newspaper articles and articles from well-known reference works are not usually included in Chicago Style bibliographies, the Wikipedia, *Oxford English Dictionary*, and *Vancouver Sun* articles are not included). Ignore initial articles (*the*, *a*, *an*) when alphabetizing.

Broadview Press. "Broadview's 2020 Recycled Paper Usage and Charitable Donations." Accessed May 3, 2021. https://broadviewpress.com/broadviews-2020-recycled-paper-usage-and-charitable-donations/.

Commonwealth Corporation of Massachusetts. *Resources for Individuals & Communities in Response to Coronavirus (COVID-19)*. 2020. Accessed January 12, 2021. https://archives.lib.state.ma.us/bitstream/handle/2452/831037/on1178881472.pdf?sequence=1&isAllowed=y.

Major League Baseball. *2021 Regular Season Standings*. Accessed June 9, 2021. https://www.mlb.com/standings.

9. works from a collection of readings or anthology: In the citation for a work in an anthology or collection of essays, use the name of the author of the work you are citing. If the work is reprinted in one source but was first published elsewhere, include the details of the original publication in the bibliography.

6. Eric Hobsbawm, "Peasant Land Occupations," in *Uncommon People: Resistance and Rebellion* (London: Weidenfeld & Nicolson, 1998), 167.

7. Daniel Heath Justice, "The Necessity of Nationhood: Affirming the Sovereignty of Indigenous National Literatures," in *Introduction to Indigenous Literary Criticism in Canada*, ed. Heather Macfarlane and Armand Garnet Ruffo (Peterborough, ON: Broadview Press, 2015), 245.

Hobsbawm, Eric. "Peasant Land Occupations." In *Uncommon People: Resistance and Rebellion*, 166–90. London: Weidenfeld & Nicolson, 1998. Originally published in *Past and Present* 62 (1974): 120–52.

Justice, Daniel Heath. "The Necessity of Nationhood: Affirming the Sovereignty of Indigenous National Literatures." In *Introduction to Indigenous Literary Criticism in Canada*, edited by Heather Macfarlane and Armand Garnet Ruffo, 241–55. Peterborough, ON: Broadview Press, 2015. Originally published in *Moveable Margins*, edited by Chelva Kanaganayakam. Toronto: TSAR Publications, 2005.

Chicago Style

10. indirect source: If you are citing a source from a reference other than the original source itself, you should include information about both sources, supplying as much information as you are able to about the original source.

- In de Beauvoir's famous phrase, "one is not born a woman, one becomes one."[1]

 1. Simone de Beauvoir, *The Second Sex* (London: Heinemann, 1966), 44, quoted in Ann Levey, "Feminist Philosophy Today," *Philosophy Now*, par. 8, accessed October 8, 2020, http://www.ucalgary.ca.philosophy.nowsite675.html.

de Beauvoir, Simone. *The Second Sex.* London: Heinemann, 1966. Quoted in Ann Levey, "Feminist Philosophy Today," *Philosophy Now*. Accessed October 8, 2020. http://www.ucalgary.ca.philosophy.nowsite675.html.

11. two or more works by the same author: After the first entry in the bibliography, use three hyphens to begin subsequent entries of works by the same author (rather than repeat the author's name). Entries for multiple works by the same author are normally arranged alphabetically by title.

Menand, Louis. "Bad Comma: Lynne Truss's Strange Grammar." *The New Yorker,* June 28, 2004. http://www.newyorker.com/critics/books/?040628crbo_books1.
---. *The Metaphysical Club: A Story of Ideas in America.* New York: Knopf, 2002.

12. edited works: Entries for edited works include the abbreviation *ed.* or *eds.* Note that when *ed.* appears after a title, it means "edited by."

 5. Roberto Frega and Steven Levine, eds., *John Dewey's Ethical Theory: The 1932 Ethics* (London: Routledge, 2021), 256.

6. Mary Shelley, *Frankenstein*, 3rd ed., ed. Lorne Macdonald and Kathleen Scherf, Broadview Editions (Peterborough, ON: Broadview Press, 2012), 89.

Frega, Roberto, and Steven Levine, eds. *John Dewey's Ethical Theory: The 1932 Ethics*. London: Routledge, 2021.

Shelley, Mary. *Frankenstein*. 3rd ed. Edited by Lorne Macdonald and Kathleen Scherf. Broadview Editions. Peterborough, ON: Broadview Press, 2012.

13. translated works: The name of the translator follows the work's title. Notice that, in the first example below, the work's author is unknown; begin with the author's name if it is known.

1. *Beowulf*, trans. R.M. Liuzza, 2nd ed. (Peterborough, ON: Broadview Press, 2012), 91.

2. Franz Kafka, "A Hunger Artist," *The Metamorphosis and Other Stories*, trans. Ian Johnston (Peterborough, ON: Broadview Press, 2015), 112.

Beowulf. Translated by R. M. Liuzza. 2nd ed. Peterborough, ON: Broadview Press, 2012.

Kafka, Franz. "A Hunger Artist." *The Metamorphosis and Other Stories*. Translated by Ian Johnston. Peterborough, ON: Broadview Press, 2015.

14. e-books: Electronic books come in several formats. The first of the two sample citations below is for a book found online; the second is for a book downloaded onto an e-reader.

4. Mary Roberts Rinehart, *Tish* (1916; Project Gutenberg, 2005), chap. 2, http://www.gutenberg.org/catalog/world/readfile?fk_files=1452441.

5. Lao Tzu, *Tao Te Ching: A Book about the Way and the Power of the Way*, trans. Ursula K. Le Guin (Boston: Shambhala, 2011), verse 12, iBooks.

Lao Tzu. *Tao Te Ching: A Book about the Way and the Power of the Way.* Translated by Ursula K. Le Guin. Boston: Shambhala, 2011. iBooks.

Rinehart, Mary Roberts. *Tish.* 1916. Project Gutenberg, 2005. http://www.gutenberg.org/catalog/world/readfile?fk_files=1452441.

15. magazine articles: The titles of articles appear in quotation marks. If no authorship is attributed, list the title of the article as the "author" in the footnote, and, if a bibliography entry is deemed necessary, the magazine title may be listed there as "author." Specific page references should be included in notes, but page ranges for magazine articles may be omitted from the bibliography.

2. Ferdinand Mount, "Ruthless and Truthless," *London Review of Books*, May 6, 2021, 7.

3. "The Impact of Green Investors," *Economist*, March 27, 2021, https://www.economist.com/finance-and-economics/2021/03/27/the-impact-of-green-investors.

4. Alec MacGillis, "The Union Battle at Amazon Is Far from Over," *New Yorker*, April 13, 2021, https://www.newyorker.com/news/news-desk/the-union-battle-at-amazon-is-far-from-over.

Economist. "The Impact of Green Investors." March 27, 2021. https://www.economist.com/finance-and-economics/2021/03/27/the-impact-of-green-investors.

MacGillis, Alec. "The Union Battle at Amazon Is Far from Over." *New Yorker*, April 13, 2021. https://www.newyorker.com/news/news-desk/the-union-battle-at-amazon-is-far-from-over.

Mount, Ferdinand. "Ruthless and Truthless." *London Review of Books*, May 6, 2021.

16. newspaper articles: The basic principles to follow with newspaper articles or editorials are the same as with magazine articles (see above). Give page numbers in the note if your source is a hard copy rather than an electronic version, but indicate section designation alone in the bibliography entry.

1. Konrad Yakabuski, "Many Looking for Meaning in Vice-Presidential Debate," *The Globe and Mail*, October 12, 2012, A3.

2. Emma Graney and Jeffrey Jones, "Big Oil Loses Carbon Emissions Showdown in Landmark Case," *Globe and Mail*, May 26, 2021, https://www.theglobeandmail.com/business/article-canadas-oil-industry-on-watch-after-dutch-court-orders-shell-to-cut/.

Graney, Emma, and Jeffrey Jones. "Big Oil Loses Carbon Emissions Showdown in Landmark Case." *Globe and Mail*, May 26, 2021. https://www.theglobeandmail.com/business/article-canadas-oil-industry-on-watch-after-dutch-court-orders-shell-to-cut/.

Yakabuski, Konrad. "Many Looking for Meaning in Vice-Presidential Debate." *The Globe and Mail*, October 12, 2012, sec. A.

17. journal articles: The basic principles are the same as with magazine articles, but volume number, and issue number (if the journal is published more than once a year), should be included as well as the date. Give page numbers or e-locator numbers where available. For online journal articles, provide the DOI, if available, rather than the URL.

1. Amy Y. Li, "The Weight of the Metric: Performance Funding and the Retention of Historically Underserved Students," *The Journal of Higher Education* 90, no. 6 (April

2019): 970–71, https://doi.org/10.1080/00221546.2019
.1602391.

2. Amanda L. Griffith and Veronica Sovero, "Under
Pressure: How Faculty Gender and Contract Uncertainty
Impact Students' Grades," *Economics of Education Review*
83 (May 2021): 6, e102126, https://doi.org/10.1016/
j.econedurev.2021.102126.

3. Esteban M. Aucejo et al., "The Impact of COVID-19 on
Student Experiences and Expectations: Evidence from a Survey," *Journal of Public Economics* 191 (November 2020): 2–3,
e104271, https://doi.org/10.1016/j.jpubeco.2020.104271.

Aucejo, Esteban M., Jacob French, Maria Paola Ugalde
Araya, and Basil Zafar. "The Impact of COVID-19 On
Student Experiences and Expectations: Evidence from
a Survey." *Journal of Public Economics* 191 (November
2020): e104271. https://doi.org/10.1016/j.jpubeco
.2020.104271.

Griffith, Amanda L., and Veronica Sovero. "Under Pressure:
How Faculty Gender and Contract Uncertainty Impact
Students' Grades." *Economics of Education Review*
83 (May 2021): e102126. https://doi.org/10.1016/
j.econedurev.2021.102126.

Li, Amy Y. "The Weight of the Metric: Performance Funding and the Retention of Historically Underserved Students." *The Journal of Higher Education* 90, no. 6 (April
2019): 965–91. https://doi.org/10.1080/00221546
.2019.1602391.

18. films and video recordings: Include the director's
name, the city of production, the production company,
and date. Depending on the context, you may wish to add
further details (actors, writers, producers) to the author section of the citation. Add the medium of publication if the

film is recorded on DVD or videocassette; if it is streamed online, add the air date and URL.

> 1. *The Birds,* directed by Alfred Hitchcock (1963; Los Angeles: Universal Studios Home Entertainment, 2005), DVD.
> 2. *Nomadland,* directed by Chloé Zhao, featuring Frances McDormand (Los Angeles: Searchlight Pictures, 2020), on Hulu, https://www.hulu.com/nomadland-movie.

Hitchcock, Alfred, dir. *The Birds.* 1963; Los Angeles: Universal Studios Home Entertainment, 2005. DVD.
Zhao, Chloé, dir. *Nomadland.* Featuring Frances McDormand. Los Angeles: Searchlight Pictures, 2020, on Hulu. https://www.hulu.com/nomadland-movie.

19. television broadcasts: To cite an episode, start with the title of the show; then give the episode number, broadcast date, and network. Include the names of the relevant contributors. The bibliography entry should be listed under the director's name.

> 1. *Little Fires Everywhere*, season 1, episode 1, "The Spark," directed by Lynn Shelton, written by Liz Tigelaar, aired March 18, 2020, on Hulu, https://www.hulu.com/series/little-fires-everywhere-bce24897-1a74-48a3-95e8-6cdd530dde4c.

Shelton, Lynn, dir. *Little Fires Everywhere.* Season 1, episode 1, "The Spark." Written by Liz Tigelaar. Aired March 18, 2020, on Hulu. https://www.hulu.com/series/little-fires-everywhere-bce24897-1a74-48a3-95e8-6cdd530dde4c.

20. sound recordings: Include the original date of recording if it is different from the recording release date, as well as the recording number and medium.

Chicago Style

1. Glenn Gould, performance of *Goldberg Variations*, by Johann Sebastian Bach, recorded 1981, CBS MK 37779, 1982, compact disc.

Gould, Glenn. Performance of *Goldberg Variations*. By Johann Sebastian Bach. Recorded 1981. CBS MK 37779, 1982, compact disc.

21. interviews and personal communications: Notes and bibliography entries begin with the name of the person interviewed. Only interviews that are broadcast, published, or available online appear in the bibliography.

7. Claudia Rankine, "The Art of Poetry No. 102," interview by David L. Ulin, *Paris Review*, no. 219 (Winter 2016), accessed February 20, 2021, https://www.theparisreview.org/interviews/6905/the-art-of-poetry-no-102-claudia-rankine.

8. Patricia Lockwood, "Patricia Lockwood Is a Good Reason to Never Log Off," interview by Gabriella Paiella, *GQ*, February 15, 2021, accessed April 2, 2021, https://www.gq.com/story/patricia-lockwood-book-interview.

9. Willie Nelson, "The Silver-Headed Stranger," interview by Andrew Goldman, *New York Times Magazine*, December 16, 2012, 12.

10. Herbert Rosengarten, telephone interview by author, January 17, 2020.

Lockwood, Patricia. "Patricia Lockwood Is a Good Reason to Never Log Off." Interview by Gabriella Paiella. *GQ*, February 15, 2021. Accessed April 2, 2021. https://www.gq.com/story/patricia-lockwood-book-interview.

Nelson, Willie. "The Silver-Headed Stranger." Interview by Andrew Goldman. *New York Times Magazine*, December 16, 2012, 12.

Rankine, Claudia. "The Art of Poetry No. 102." Interview by David L. Ulin. *Paris Review*, no. 219 (Winter 2016). Accessed February 20, 2021. https://www.theparisreview.org/interviews/6905/the-art-of-poetry-no-102-claudia-rankine.

22. book reviews: The name of the reviewer (if it has been provided) should come first, as shown below:

1. Brian Leiter and Michael Weisberg, "Do You Only Have a Brain? On Thomas Nagel," review of *Why the Materialist Neo-Darwinian Conception of Nature Is Almost Certainly False*, by Thomas Nagel, *The Nation*, October 22, 2012, http://www.thenation.com/article/170334/do-you-only-have-brain-thomas-nagel.

Leiter, Brian, and Michael Weisberg. "Do You Only Have a Brain? On Thomas Nagel." Review of *Why the Materialist Neo-Darwinian Conception of Nature Is Almost Certainly False*, by Thomas Nagel. *The Nation*, October 22, 2012. http://www.thenation.com/article/170334/do-you-only-have-brain-thomas-nagel.

23. blog posts: Begin with the author's name, if there is one.

1. Tom Clayton, "York School Crowdfunds for 'Magical' Reading Cottage," *MobyLives* (blog), May 18, 2021, https://www.mhpbooks.com/york-school-crowdfunds-for-magical-reading-cottage/.

Clayton, Tom. "York School Crowdfunds for 'Magical' Reading Cottage." *MobyLives* (blog), May 18, 2021. https://www.mhpbooks.com/york-school-crowdfunds-for-magical-reading-cottage/.

24. websites: Unless the website title is also that of a book or periodical, do not put the site's title in italics. If possible, indicate when the site was last updated; otherwise, include your date of access.

> 1. The Camelot Project, University of Rochester, last modified December 21, 2012, http://www.lib.rochester.edu/camelot/cphome.stm.

> The Camelot Project. University of Rochester. Last modified December 21, 2012. http://www.lib.rochester.edu/camelot/cphome.stm.

25. online videos: Include the author or principal performer, length of the video, and date of posting, if available, as well as the medium and its source.

> 1. Anindya Kundu, "The 'Opportunity Gap' in US Public Education," TED video, January 23, 2020, 5:33, https://www.youtube.com/watch?v=wRG5_-9eE4w.

> Kundu, Anindya. "The 'Opportunity Gap' in US Public Education." TED video. January 23, 2020. https://www.youtube.com/watch?v=wRG5_-9eE4w.

26. tweets: Chicago Style recommends that a tweet be fully transcribed (up to 160 characters). This can happen in your note or in the text of your essay (see the examples below). If you include the tweet and citation information in the body of your essay, you may omit a note. In most cases, you need not include a bibliography entry for a tweet, but if you are citing the tweet more than once, or if it is an extended thread, then you may wish to create an entry. Note that, like all websites that don't have a print counterpart, Twitter is not italicized; note also that time stamps should be included in both the note and bibliography entry.

- On May 17, 2021, Stephen King tweeted about the elusive nature of artistic inspiration: "Good writing is a delight to those who read it and a mystery to those who write it."

1. Stephen King (@StephenKing), "Good writing is a delight to those who read it and a mystery to those who write it," Twitter, May 17, 2021, 9:10 p.m., https://twitter.com/StephenKing/status/1394460364549627906.

King, Stephen (@StephenKing). "Good writing is a delight to those who read it and a mystery to those who write it." Twitter, May 17, 2021, 9:10 p.m. https://twitter.com/StephenKing/status/1394460364549627906.

Among the details to notice in this reference system:

- Where two or more works by the same author are included in the bibliography, they are normally arranged alphabetically by title.
- All major words in titles and subtitles are capitalized.
- Date of publication must appear, where known. Provision of your date of access to electronic materials may be helpful, but is not required.
- Commas are used to separate elements within a footnote, and, in many circumstances, periods separate these same elements in the bibliographic entry.
- When a work has appeared in an edited collection, information on the editors must be included in both the first note and the bibliographic reference.
- First author's first and last names are reversed in the bibliography.
- Translators must be noted both in footnotes and in the bibliography.
- Publisher as well as city of publication should be given.

Chicago Style

- Months and publisher names are not abbreviated.
- The day of the month comes after the name of the month.
- Online references should include a publication date, if available, and/or a revision date. You may also include both: "Published June 10, 2019; last modified February 3, 2021." If neither date is available, include the access date: "Accessed March 2, 2021."

○ *Chicago Style Sample*

A sample of text with citations in Chicago style appears below. Note that a full sample essay in Chicago style appears on the adjunct website associated with this book.

Urban renewal is as much a matter of psychology as it is of bricks and mortar. As Paul Goldberger has described, there have been many plans to revitalize Havana.[1] But both that city and the community of Cuban exiles in Florida remain haunted by a sense of absence and separation. As Lourdes Casal reminds us,

> Exile
>
> is living where there is no house whatever in
>
> which we were ever children …[2]

The psychology of outsiders also makes a difference. Part of the reason Americans have not much noticed the dire plight of their fifth-largest city is that it does not "stir the national imagination."[3] Conversely, there has been far more concern over the state of cities such as New Orleans and Quebec City, whose history and architecture excite the romantic imagination. As Nora Phelps has discussed, the past is in itself a key trigger for romantic notions, and it is no doubt inevitable that cities whose history is particularly visible will engender passionate attachments.[4] And as Stephanie Wright and

---

1. Paul Goldberger, "Annals of Preservation: Bringing Back Havana," *The New Republic*, January 2005, 54, accessed March 4, 2020, http://www.findarticles.comgoldberg.p65.jn.htm.

2. Lourdes Casal, "Definition," trans. Elizabeth Macklin, *The New Yorker*, January 26, 1998, 79.

3. Witold Rybczynski, "The Fifth City," review of *A Prayer for the City*, by Buzz Bissinger, *New York Review of Books*, February 5, 1998, 13.

4. Nora Phelps, "Pastness and the Foundations of Romanticism," *Romanticism on the Net* 11 (May 2001): par. 14, accessed March 4, 2020, http://users.ox.ac.uk/~scato385/phelpsmws.htm.

Carole King have detailed in an important case study,[1] almost all French-speaking Quebecers feel their heritage to be bound up with that of Quebec City. (Richard Ford's character Frank Bascombe has suggested that "New Orleans defeats itself" by longing "for a mystery it doesn't have and never will, if it ever did,"[2] but this remains a minority view.)

In addition to the roles history and memory play in shaping our approach to urban renewal, new research also points to the crucial impact of nature experience on psychological health. This has prompted urban designers, city planners, and psychologists to prioritize access to green and blue spaces in their design plans for cities. One important dimension of this emergent research is environmental justice; as one study of Los Angeles's San Fernando Valley concludes, "We find that low-income neighborhoods … have higher traffic volumes, fewer shade trees, and street environments that are less clean and well maintained compared to high-income areas and that similar disparities exist between ethnic minority and white communities."[3] A just vision of urban revitalization would include prioritizing access to natural environments for all members of the community.

---

1. Stephanie Wright and Carole King, *Quebec: A History*, 2 vols. (Montreal: McGill-Queen's University Press, 2012).

2. Richard Ford, *The Sportswriter*, 2nd ed. (New York: Random House, 1995), 48.

3. Alessandro Rigolon, Zeynep Toker, and Nara Gasparian, "Who Has More Walkable Routes to Parks? An Environmental Justice Study of Safe Routes to Parks in Neighborhoods of Los Angeles," *Journal of Urban Affairs* 40, no. 4 (2018): 576, https://doi.org/10.1080/07352166.2017.1360740.

The bibliography relating to the above text would be as follows:

Bibliography

Casal, Lourdes. "Definition." Translated by Elizabeth Macklin. *The New Yorker*, January 26, 1998, 79.

Ford, Richard. *The Sportswriter*. 2nd ed. New York: Random House, 1995.

Goldberger, Paul. "Annals of Preservation: Bringing Back Havana." *The New Yorker*, January 26, 2005, 50–62. http://www.findarticles.com.goldberg.p65.jn.htm.

Phelps, Nora. "Pastness and the Foundations of Romanticism." *Romanticism on the Net* 11 (May 2001). http://users.ox.ac.uk/~scat0385/phelpsmws.htm.

Rigolon, Alessandro, Zeynep Toker, and Nara Gasparian. "Who Has More Walkable Routes to Parks? An Environmental Justice Study of Safe Routes to Parks in Neighborhoods of Los Angeles." *Journal of Urban Affairs* 40, no. 4 (2018): 576–91. https://doi.org/10.1080/07352166.2017.1360740.

Rybczynski, Witold. "The Fifth City." Review of *A Prayer for the City*, by Buzz Bissinger. *New York Review of Books*, February 5, 1998, 12–14.

Wright, Stephanie, and Carole King. *Quebec: A History*. 2 vols. Montreal: McGill-Queen's University Press, 2012.

CSE Style

In-Text Citation   213
    citation-name format   213
    citation-sequence format   214
    name-year format   214
List of References   214
    citation-name format   214
    citation-sequence format   215
    name-year format   215
CSE Style Samples   217
    citation-name format   217
    citation-sequence format   221
    name-year format   225

CSE Style

CSE Style

The Council of Science Editors (CSE) style of documentation is commonly used in the natural sciences and the physical sciences. Guidelines are set out in *Scientific Style and Format: The CSE Manual for Authors, Editors, and Publishers*, 8th ed. (2014). The key features of CSE style are outlined below, and short sample essays using the three formats of the CSE documentation system follow at the end of this section.

In-Text Citation: Citations in CSE style may follow three alternative formats: a **citation-name** format, a **citation-sequence** format, or a **name-year** format.

In the **citation-name** format, a reference list is compiled and arranged alphabetically by author. Each reference is then assigned a number in sequence, with the first alphabetical entry receiving the number 1, the second the number 2, and so on. Whenever you refer in your text to the reference labeled with number 3, for example, you use either a superscript number 3 (in one variation) or the number 3 in parentheses (in another).

- The difficulties first encountered in this experiment have been accounted for, according to Zelinsky[3]. However, the variables still have not been sufficiently well controlled for this type of experiment, argues Gibson[1].
- The difficulties first encountered in this experiment have been accounted for, according to Zelinsky (3). However, the variables still have not been sufficiently well controlled for this type of experiment, argues Gibson (1).

In the **citation-sequence** format, superscript numbers (or numbers in parentheses) are inserted after the mention of any source. The first source mentioned receives number 1, the second number 2, and so on.

- The difficulties first encountered in this experiment have been accounted for, according to Zelinsky[1]. However, the variables still have not been sufficiently well controlled for this type of experiment, argues Gibson[2].
- The difficulties first encountered in this experiment have been accounted for, according to Zelinsky (1). However, the variables still have not been sufficiently well controlled for this type of experiment, argues Gibson (2).

Reuse the number you first assign to a source whenever you refer to it again.

In the **name-year** format, you cite the author surname and year of publication in parentheses:

- The key contributions to the study of variables in the 2000s (Gibson et al. 2008; Soames 2009; Zelinsky 2007) have been strongly challenged in recent years.

For two authors, list both, separated by *and*; for more than two authors, give the first author's surname, followed by *et al.*

List of References: Citations in CSE style must correspond to items in a list of References.

In the **citation-name** format, entries are arranged alphabetically and assigned a number.

1. Gibson DL, Lampman GM, Kriz FR, Taylor DM. Introduction to statistical techniques in the sciences. 2nd ed. New York: MacQuarrie Learning; 2008. 1254 p.
2. Soames G. Variables in large database experiments. J Nat Hist. 2009; 82: 1811–41.
3. Zelinsky KL. The study of variables: an overview. New York: Academic; 2007. 216 p.

In the **citation-sequence** format, the references are listed in the sequence in which they have been cited in the text.

1. Zelinsky KL. The study of variables: an overview. New York: Academic; 2007. 216 p.
2. Gibson DL, Lampman GM, Kriz FR, Taylor DM. Introduction to statistical techniques in the sciences. 2nd ed. New York: MacQuarrie Learning; 2008. 1254 p.
3. Soames G. Variables in large database experiments. J Nat Hist. 2009; 82: 1811–41.

In the **name-year** format, the references are listed alphabetically, and the year of publication is given prominence.

Gibson DL, Lampman GM, Kriz FR, Taylor DM. 2008. Introduction to statistical techniques in the sciences. 2nd ed. New York: MacQuarrie Learning. 1254 p.

Soames G. 2009. Variables in large database experiments. J Nat Hist. 82: 1811–41.

Zelinsky KL. 2007. The study of variables: an overview. New York: Academic. 216 p.

The basic principles of the system are the same regardless of whether one is citing a book, an article in a journal or magazine, a newspaper article, or an electronic document. Here are the main details.

Author names in the References list are all inverted, with initials given instead of full first names. Initials have

CSE Style

no periods after them, and no commas separate them from surnames. If a source in the References list has two to ten authors, include all of them; do not include *and* at any point in the list. For more than ten authors, give the names of the first ten, with *and others* following the last one listed.

Capitalize all major words in the titles of periodicals (journals, magazines, and newspapers). For books and articles, capitalize only the first word of the title, as well as any proper nouns. Abbreviate journal titles according to standardized guidelines. You can find the accepted abbreviation of a journal title at the Genamics JournalSeek site online (http://journalseek.net/); enter the journal's full title into the *Search Title* field.

Entries for books include the city of publication, the publisher, and the date of publication.

Entries for periodical articles should include the date: for journal articles, give the year; for magazine articles, give the year and month (abbreviated); for newspaper articles, give the year, the month (abbreviated), and the day.

For online sources, include all of the publication information that you would for print sources. The position of the date of access (e.g., *accessed 2013 Feb 13*) varies according to which format you use. Give the URL or DOI following the date of access. Do not put a period at the end of a DOI or a URL (unless it ends with a slash).

CSE Style Samples

The following is written using the **citation-name** format.

Over the centuries scientific study has evolved into several distinct disciplines. Physics, chemistry, and biology were established early on; in the nineteenth and twentieth centuries they were joined by others, such as geology and ecology. Much as the disciplines have their separate spheres, the sphere of each overlaps those of others. This may be most obvious in the case of ecology, which some have claimed to be a discipline that makes a holistic approach to science respectable[2]. In the case of geology, as soon as it became clear in the nineteenth century that the fossil record of geological life would be central to the future of geology, the importance of connecting with the work of biologists became recognized[7]. Nowadays it is not surprising to have geological research conducted jointly by biologists and geologists (e.g., Newton, Trewman, and Elser[8]). And, with the acceptance of "continental drift" theories in the 1960s and 1970s, physics came to be increasingly relied on for input into discussions of such topics as collision tectonics (e.g., Escuder-Viruete and Pérez[5]).

The growth of the subdiscipline of biochemistry at the point of overlap between biology and chemistry is well known, but many are unaware that the scope of biological physics is almost as broad; Frauenfrommer[6] provides a helpful survey. Today it is not uncommon, indeed, to see research such as the recent study by Corel, Marks, and Hutner[4] or that by Balmberg,

Passano, and Proule[1], both of which draw on biology, chemistry, and physics simultaneously.

Interdisciplinary scientific exploration has also been spurred by the growth of connections between the pure and applied sciences such as meteorology, as recent research into such topics as precipitation[3] confirms. But to the extent that science is driven by the applied, will it inextricably become more and more driven by commercial concerns? David Resnik[9] thinks there are measures we can take to limit financial influences on scientific integrity.

The citations above would connect to References as follows:

References

1. Balmberg NJ, Passano C, Proule AB. The Lorenz-Fermi-Pasta-Ulam experiment. Physica D. 2005 [accessed 2020 Mar 7]; 138(1): 1–47. Available from: http://www.elseviere.com/locate/phys

2. Branmer A. Ecology in the twentieth century: a history. New Haven: Yale UP; 2004. 320 p.

3. Caine JS, Gross SM, Baldwin G. Melting effect as a factor in precipitation-type forecasting. Weather Forecast. 2010; 15(6): 700–14.

4. Corel B, Marks VJ, Hutner H. The modelling effect of Elpasolites. Chem Sci. 2013; 55(10): 935–38.

5. Escuder-Viruete J, Pérez Y. Neotectonic structures and stress fields associated with oblique collision and forearc sliver formation in northern Hispaniola: implications for the seismic hazard assessment. Tectonophysics. 2020 [accessed 2021 May 5]; 784(228452): doi:10.1016/j.tecto.2020.228452

6. Frauenfrommer H. Introduction. In Frauenfrommer H, Hum G, Glazer RG, editors. Biological physics third international symposium; 1998 Mar 8–9; Santa Fe, NM [Melville, NY]: American Institute of Physics. 386 p.

7. Lyell C. Principles of geology. London: John Murray; 1830. 588 p.

8. Newton MJ, Trewman NH, Elser S. A new jawless invertebrate from the Middle Devonian. Paleontology. 2011 [accessed 2020 Mar 5]; 44(1): 43–52. doi:10.1136/p.330.6500.442

9. Resnik D. Science and money: problems and solutions. J Microbiol Biol Educ. 2014 [accessed 2021 May 4]; 15(2): 159–61. doi:10.1128/jmbe.v15i2.792

Among the details to notice in the citation-name format of the CSE style:

- The entries in References are numbered and listed in alphabetical order according to author.

- Unpunctuated initials rather than first names are used in References.

- The date appears near the end of the reference, before any page reference.

- Only the first words of titles are capitalized (except for proper nouns and the abbreviated titles of journals).

- When a work has appeared in an edited collection the names of the editor(s) as well as the author(s) must appear in the reference.

- Publisher as well as city of publication should be given.

- Months and journal names are generally abbreviated.

- References to electronic publications include the date of access as well as date of publication or latest revision.

- Names of articles appear with no surrounding quotation marks; names of books and journal titles appear with no italics.

Here is the same passage with the CSE **citation-sequence** format used:

Over the centuries scientific study has evolved into several distinct disciplines. Physics, chemistry, and biology were established early on; in the nineteenth and twentieth centuries they were joined by others, such as geology and ecology. Much as the disciplines have their separate spheres, the sphere of each overlaps those of others. This may be most obvious in the case of ecology, which some have claimed to be a discipline that makes a holistic approach to science respectable[1]. In the case of geology, as soon as it became clear in the nineteenth century that the fossil record of geological life would be central to the future of geology, the importance of connecting with the work of biologists became recognized[2]. Nowadays it is not surprising to have geological research conducted jointly by biologists and geologists (e.g., the work of Newton, Trewman, and Elser[3]). And, with the acceptance of "continental drift" theories in the 1960s and 1970s, physics came to be increasingly relied on for input into discussions of such topics as collision tectonics (e.g., Escuder-Viruete and Pérez[4]).

The growth of the subdiscipline of biochemistry at the point of overlap between biology and chemistry is well known, but many are unaware that the scope of biological physics is almost as broad; Frauenfrommer[5] provides a helpful survey. Today it is not uncommon, indeed, to see research such as the recent study by Corel, Marks, and Hutner[6], or that by Balmberg, Passano, and Proule[7], both of which draw on biology, chemistry, and physics simultaneously.

Interdisciplinary scientific exploration has also been spurred by the growth of connections between the pure and applied sciences such as meteorology, as recent research into such topics as precipitation[8] confirms. But to the extent that science is driven by the applied, will it inextricably become more and more driven by commercial concerns? David Resnik thinks there are measures we can take to limit financial influences on scientific integrity.[9]

CSE Style

The citations above would connect to References as follows:

References

1. Branmer A. Ecology in the twentieth century: a history. New Haven: Yale UP; 2004. 320 p.

2. Lyell C. Principles of geology. London: John Murray; 1830. 588 p.

3. Newton MJ, Trewman NH, Elser S. A new jawless invertebrate from the Middle Devonian. Paleontology. 2011 [accessed 2020 Mar 5]; 44(1): 43–52. doi:10.1136/p.330.6500.442

4. Escuder-Viruete J, Pérez Y. Neotectonic structures and stress fields associated with oblique collision and forearc sliver formation in northern Hispaniola: implications for the seismic hazard assessment. Tectonophysics. 2020 [accessed 2021 May 5]; 784(228452): doi:10.1016/j.tecto.2020.228452

5. Frauenfrommer H. Introduction. In: Frauenfrommer H, Hum G, Glazer RG, editors. Biological physics third international symposium; 1998 Mar 8–9; Santa Fe, NM [Melville, NY]: American Institute of Physics. 386 p.

6. Corel B, Marks VJ, Hutner H. The modelling effect of Elpasolites. Chem Sci. 2013; 55(10): 935–38.

7. Balmberg NJ, Passano C, Proule AB. The Lorenz-Fermi-Pasta-Ulam experiment. Physica D. 2005 [accessed 2020 Mar 7]; 138(1): 1–47. http://www.elseviere.com/locate/phys

8. Caine JS, Gross SM, Baldwin G. Melting effect as a factor in precipitation-type forecasting. Weather Forecast. 2010; 15(6): 700–14.

9. Resnik D. Science and money: problems and solutions. J Microbiol Biol Educ. 2014 [accessed 2021 May 4]; 15(2): 159–61. doi:10.1128/jmbe.v15i2.792

Among the details to notice in the citation-sequence format of the CSE style:

- The entries in References are listed in the order they first appear in the text.

- Unpunctuated initials rather than first names are used in References.

- The date appears near the end of the reference, before any page reference.

- Only the first words of titles are capitalized (except for proper nouns and the abbreviated titles of journals).

- When a work has appeared in an edited collection the names of the editor(s) as well as the author(s) must appear in the reference.

- Publisher as well as city of publication should be given.

- Months and journal names are generally abbreviated.

- References to electronic publications include the date of access as well as date of publication or latest revision.

- Names of articles appear with no surrounding quotation marks; names of books and journal titles appear with no italics.

Here is the same passage again, this time using the CSE **name-year** format:

Over the centuries scientific study has evolved into several distinct disciplines. Physics, chemistry, and biology were established early on; in the nineteenth and twentieth centuries, they were joined by others, such as geology and ecology. Much as the disciplines have their separate spheres, the sphere of each overlaps those of others. This may be most obvious in the case of ecology, which some have claimed to be a discipline that makes a holistic approach to science respectable (Branmer 2004). In the case of geology, as soon as it became clear in the nineteenth century that the fossil record of geological life would be central to the future of geology, the importance of connecting with the work of biologists became recognized (Lyell 1830). Nowadays it is not surprising to have geological research conducted jointly by biologists and geologists (e.g., Newton, Trewman, and Elser 2011). And, with the acceptance of "continental drift" theories in the 1960s and 1970s, physics came to be increasingly relied on for input into discussions of such topics as collision tectonics (e.g., Escuder-Viruete and Pérez 2020).

The growth of the subdiscipline of biochemistry at the point of overlap between biology and chemistry is well known, but many are unaware that the scope of biological physics is almost as broad; Frauenfrommer (1998) provides a helpful survey. Today it is not uncommon, indeed, to see research such as the recent study by Corel, Marks, and Hutner (2013) or that by Balmberg, Passano, and Proule (2005), both of which draw on biology, chemistry, and physics simultaneously.

Interdisciplinary scientific exploration has also been spurred by the growth of connections between the pure and applied sciences such as meteorology, as recent research into such topics as precipitation (Caine, Gross, and Baldwin 2010) confirms. But to the extent that science is driven by the applied, will it inextricably become more and more driven by commercial concerns? David Resnik (2014) thinks there are measures we can take to limit financial influences on scientific integrity.

The citations above would connect to References as follows:

References

Balmberg NJ, Passano C, Proule AB. 2005. The Lorenz-Fermi-Pasta-Ulam experiment. Physica D. [accessed 2020 Mar 7]; 138(1): 1–47. Available from: http://www.elseviere.com/locate/phys

Branmer A. 2004. Ecology in the twentieth century: a history. New Haven: Yale UP. 320 p.

Caine JS, Gross SM, Baldwin G. 2010. Melting effect as a factor in precipitation-type forecasting. Weather Forecast. 15(6): 700–14.

Corel B, Marks VJ, Hutner H. 2013. The modelling effect of Elpaso-lites. Chem Sci. 55(10): 935–38.

Escuder-Viruete J, Pérez Y. 2020. Neotectonic structures and stress fields associated with oblique collision and forearc sliver formation in northern Hispaniola: implications for the seismic hazard assessment. Tectonophysics. [accessed 2021 May 5]; 784(228452). doi:10.1016/j.tecto.2020.228452

Frauenfrommer H. Introduction. In: Frauenfrommer H, Hum G, Glazer RG, editors. 1998 Mar 8–9. Biological physics third international symposium. Santa Fe, NM [Melville, NY]: American Institute of Physics. 386 p.

Lyell C. 1830. Principles of geology. London: John Murray. 588 p.

Newton MJ, Trewman NH, Elser S. 2011. A new jawless invertebrate from the Middle Devonian. Paleontology. [accessed 2020 Mar 5]; 44(1): 43–52. doi:10.1136/p.330.6500.442

Resnik D. Science and money: problems and solutions. 2014. J Microbiol Biol Educ. [accessed 2021 May 4]; 15(2): 159–61. doi:10.1128/jmbe.v15i2.792

Among the details to notice in the name-year format of the CSE style:

- The entries in References are listed in alphabetical order by author.

- Unpunctuated initials rather than first names are used in References.

- The date appears immediately after the author name(s) at the beginning of the reference.

- The in-text citation comes before the period or comma in the surrounding sentence.

- Only the first words of titles are capitalized (except for proper nouns and the abbreviated titles of journals).

- When a work has appeared in an edited collection the names of the editor(s) as well as the author(s) must appear in the reference.

- The word *and* is used for in-text citations of works with more than one author—but not in the corresponding reference list entry.

- Publisher as well as city of publication should be given.

- Months and journal names are generally abbreviated.

- References to electronic publications include the date of access as well as the date of publication or latest revision.

- Names of articles appear with no surrounding quotation marks; names of books, journals, etc. appear with no italics.

From the Publisher

A name never says it all, but the word "Broadview" expresses a good deal of the philosophy behind our company. We are open to a broad range of academic approaches and political viewpoints. We pay attention to the broad impact book publishing and book printing has in the wider world; for some years now we have used 100% recycled paper for most titles. Our publishing program is internationally oriented and broad-ranging. Our individual titles often appeal to a broad readership too; many are of interest as much to general readers as to academics and students.

Founded in 1985, Broadview remains a fully independent company owned by its shareholders—not an imprint or subsidiary of a larger multinational.

To order our books or obtain up-to-date information, please visit www.broadviewpress.com.

broadview press
www.broadviewpress.com